MW00558814

HAUNTED
NEW
BRAUNFELS

HAUNTED
NEW
BRAUNFELS

A TRUE WILD WEST GHOST TOWN

ERIN O. WALLACE

HAUNTED
AMERICA

Published by Haunted America
A Division of The History Press
Charleston, SC 29403
www.historypress.net

Copyright © 2013 by Erin O. Wallace
All rights reserved

Cover: Phoenix Saloon. *Photograph by Justin LeVrier.*

First published 2013

ISBN 978.1.5402.0789.0

Library of Congress CIP data applied for

Dedicated to Marguerite Mae Zuercher (1910–1982), whose stories of her beloved New Braunfels inspired the author to learn more about her German ancestors.

Marguerite Mae Zuercher, descendant of Nicolas Zuercher (1804–1869), one of the original founders of New Braunfels. *Author's collection.*

CONTENTS

ACKNOWLEDGEMENTS

O n no account was the publication of *Haunted New Braunfels* an individual task. I wish to express my deepest gratitude to all who assisted me along this journey. These caring volunteers made the experience thrilling, fulfilling and memorable. First and foremost, I want to personally thank everyone who allowed their historical building to be included in this book. Their hospitality and accounts offered invaluable assistance to the project. A big thank-you goes to Christen Thompson of The History Press, whose snap of the whip was a necessary tool to keep me on track and focused. I owe an enormous group hug to my paranormal family, the Ripcrew (RIP) Researching Investigating Paranormal team, whose serious dedication to this endeavor gave crucial evidence to this work. This team consisting of founder Robbie Prince, co-founder Wiley Uzzell, April Prince, Margie Uzzell, R.J. Warren Jr., Tom Bradford and producer/investigator/my partner in crime Will Scoville tirelessly worked around my schedule, for which I am obliged. They gave up valuable family time to make certain this book received the evidence needed to be as accurate as possible. Very special thanks go to my two sisters, Mickey Cavin and Shelley Wade (who is also the case manager for Ripcrew), who continued to motivate me throughout this entire voyage. They were there by my side emotionally every step of the way. I would like to deeply thank Justin LeVrier and Ashley Ghedi LeVrier for their last-minute team effort to provide this publication with an incredible cover shot of the Phoenix Saloon (New Braunfels' most haunted building). Justin and Ashley are both talented photographers with additional cover publications on their

The Ripcrew Paranormal Team. *From left to right*: Tom Bradford, Margie Uzzel, Wiley Uzzel, Robbie Prince, Shelley Wade, April Prince and R.J. Warren Jr. *Photo by Kay Taylor.*

resumes, and I cannot thank them enough. Finally, I am forever indebted to my sweetheart, Jimmy Ghedi, for his understanding, endless patience and encouragement when it was most required. I could not have completed this without him. This was an experience I will forever cherish.

PREFACE

"Always remember it was a German prince who brought your ancestors to America. Promise to never, ever forget. You have Zuercher blood in you—this is something to be exceptionally proud of."

These were the last words I can recall my grandmother telling me before she passed away. Although it was a phrase I had heard all my life, this was the one thing she wanted to evoke in my memory before her last breath. My grandmother was the perfect example of how deep German-American pride remains within the descendants of the New Braunfels emigrants. This community-wide pride was something I knew extremely well since I spent most of my youth in Comal County. From Wurstfest, Wassail Strolling, fishing in and tubing on the Guadalupe River and fishing at Landa Park, New Braunfels offered every form of family entertainment.

As a child having heard nothing but tales of an aristocrat bringing my family to Texas and experiencing all the delightful amusements this small settlement offered, New Braunfels had become a sort of paradise in my eyes. Though located between two of the largest cities in Texas, San Antonio and Austin, I believed it had been somehow magically immune to any possibility of hostile influences or unpleasant episodes disrupting its serenity. While the citizens of this quaint town have maintained the charm and attractiveness generated by the original settlers, it has by no means been exempt from the effects of hostile beings. This became evident the moment I began searching the files of the criminal archives in the library.

Group photo of the Zuercher family. *Left to right, beginning from top*: Lena (Deininger), Emil, William, Catherine (Hohn), Augusta "Gussie" (Glaubitz) and August Zuercher, son of Nicolas and Elizabeth (Loos) Zuercher. *Author's collection.*

One reason for New Braunfels' continuous illusion of being excused from the usual illegal happenings and wrongdoings of day-to-day life was the lack of having an English-translated newspaper. Dr. Ferdinand Lindheimer (later known as the "Father of Texas Botany") had started the *Neu Braunfelser Zeitung* newspaper in 1852, but it was completely in the old German language. This kept the German-speaking community informed but not the surrounding areas that spoke mostly English. From time to time, if the event was dramatic enough, certain articles would be translated and posted in the

Lake Landa in Landa Park. Notice the paddleboat in the foreground. *Author's collection.*

The Zuercher family showing off their hunt collection while standing on the banks of the Guadalupe River. *From left to right*: Katherine Hohn Zuercher, August Zuercher, Augusta "Gussie" Zuercher, Emil Zuercher and William Zuercher. *Author's collection.*

German baptismal document of Marguerite Mae (May) Zuercher, daughter of
William and Agnes Zuercher, descendants of Nicolas and Elizabeth Zuercher.
Author's collection.

outside newspapers, but again, it had to be a rather huge crime. It wasn't
until nearly forty years later, in 1892, that another newspaper was created in
the English language, the *New Braunfels Herald*.

Before I began writing this book, I was already well informed of New
Braunfels' famous Adelsverin (Nobility Society) and many of the main

William Zuercher, descendant of Nicolas Zuercher and Agnes Goebel (1888–1970), courting in Landa Park. Notice the carriage in the background. *Author's collection.*

immigrants' names because of my upbringing. As I started my historical hauntings research, I realized that I had already been told these tales in my youth but had simply hung on to the bright side of this blissful hideaway. The more I examined the criminal archive files, the more I recalled all the haunting folklore and ghostly legends that had been passed down from my

German ancestors. This piqued my interest even more, especially being a historian, a previous paranormal author and tightly connected to a paranormal investigative team.

Some of these haunting accounts were given considerable validation with the help of the Ripcrew Paranormal Team, while select chapters relied on actual accounts from the buildings' owners as well as those of locals and longtime legends handed down throughout the years. The history is as accurate as possible, but we all know that no historical account is precise unless it was experienced firsthand. The ghost stories expressed in this publication are as close as possible to the original tales conveyed to me and what I have experienced myself. And yes, I do believe in ghosts!

THE PRINCE
WITH A DREAM

A s you stroll down the quaint streets of New Braunfels, it's easy to imagine the slower pace of days gone by. This is an old-fashioned German town that gives one a feeling of stepping back in time. The German word *willkommen*, meaning "welcome," can be seen above many local store entrances. You can still dine at *biergartens* and dance to oompah music at the Wurstfest (a German heritage celebration) in October. Even the oldest continuously operating bakery in Texas, Naegelin's, has sat on the same corner serving strudel and kolaches since 1868. The heritage of this town is so significant that the residents created an amusing sign reading, "New Braunfels, Fighting Progress Since 1848." As with most small towns, preserving its delicate history can be a daunting task. The challenge is permitting growth and improvement while still maintaining the antiquity of the buildings, and New Braunfels has seemed to achieve this thus far.

Before beginning the background history of the buildings, the present owners, their employees and locals were interviewed. At first, they were somewhat cautious about sharing their so-called paranormal experiences. One could quickly sense the hesitation in their eyes and uncomfortable body language. Getting someone to share a possible ghost sighting can be a little challenging for any author. Understandably, wondering how a paranormal encounter will be received is the biggest concern for all those involved. It also raises our own thoughts and issues of mortality and

Naegelin's Bakery, the oldest continuously running bakery in Texas. The building to the left burned down and is now a parking lot. *Author's collection.*

what lies ahead when we pass. However, once they understood that they were not alone in their concerns and bizarre meetings, they became far more relaxed in their discussions. Strangely though, as they unveiled their uncanny stories, it was obvious that each one had experienced something totally different from the other.

At first, when asked to write a book about New Braunfels, Texas, excitement was the only feeling I had—but wondering where to begin and mostly end was terrifying. This town is so steeped in history that it was difficult not to share everything possible known about this wonderful place. Then, the realization that this was purely a small collection of some of the city's ghost stories, haunting legends and unforgettable tales—not an encyclopedia of New Braunfels' history—began to set in. But it's difficult not to share more information. So the best way to resolve this is to send anyone wanting a detailed history of this fascinating German town over to the Sophienburg Museum, located in the heart of the city.

This museum has everything available to give you a true sense of what these German settlers went through. It boasts a wonderful archive and library, and the volunteers (especially Vera Seidel) there are extremely helpful. I cannot recommend a better place for a more accurate account of the German immigrants' journey to New Braunfels. With that being said, to understand these tales one must know a little bit about New Braunfels'

The Sophienburg Museum. *Author's collection.*

A drawing depicting what it would have looked like for the German settlers making their way to New Braunfels from Indianola. *Author's collection.*

beginning—so here it is in a nutshell. New Braunfels is located at the meeting of the Guadalupe and Comal Rivers and is thirty miles northeast of San Antonio and forty-five miles southwest of Austin. It was founded on March 21, 1845, when a long wagon train carrying exhausted German immigrants made camp at a site on Comal Creek.

Prince Carl of Solms-Braunfels, Germany, in his prime. *Author's collection.*

Introduction

The site was chosen by Prince Carl of Solms-Braunfels (1812–1875), who is noted for leading the establishment of colonies of German immigrants in Texas. Solms was a well-educated and well-connected handsome prince of wealth and privilege who sought adventure and looked for new worlds to explore. He was a captain in both the Austrian army and the cavalry of the Grand Duchy of Hesse in 1841. It was during his service with the cavalry that Solms read a novel by Charles Sealsfield about the newly independent Republic of Texas, as well as two other books dealing with the geography and immigration possibilities of the Lone Star Republic. Like many others before and after him, Prince Solms caught "Texas fever" and became interested in joining the Adelsverein (Noble Society). Zealously campaigning for its success, he became commissioner general of the Adelsverein. Also during this time, Solms was required to endure a royal annulment from his wife, Luise Auguste Stephanie Beyrich, as she was considered by the royalties to be below his noble station. As the prince tried to move on with his life, he devoted all his spare time as an officer of the Adelsverein. This enthusiastic and dedicated energy led him to become the motivating force for the German colony in Texas.

Solms arrived on Texas soil in July 1844 and made an exploratory tour of the republic as advisor to the Adelsverein. He was given the rights to the Fisher-Miller Land Grant. Subsequently, on behalf of the Noble Society, Solms purchased an additional 1,300 acres on the Guadalupe River, where he established the colony of New Braunfels. The contract of the immigrants with the Adelsverein stated that each head of family would receive 320 acres, with single men receiving 160 acres. When the immigrants crossed the Guadalupe to the assigned tract, they were told that they would receive only one half-acre lot and one 10-acre plot, a far cry from the original promise. A few went on to claim their Fisher/Miller land, but not many. Soon, dissatisfaction turned to acceptance when they realized the beauty and practicality of the area selected by the prince. It was on Good Friday, March 21, 1845, that what is now known as New Braunfels was officially founded.

Solms then commissioned Nicolaus Zink to plot out preliminary town and farm lots and to supervise construction of a primitive stockade to protect the immigrants against allegedly cannibalistic Indians. Within weeks, Prince Solms had laid the cornerstone for a more permanent fort and headquarters for the immigrant association on a nearby hilltop called the Sophienburg. He also made provisions for supplying the increasing settlement through its first summer on the frontier. By that summer, the settlers numbered

The caption on this postcard reads: "The Guadalupe River, one of Texas' swiftest and clearest streams, cuts a deep canyon through the mountains. The entire hilly terrain is timbered with live oak, mesquite, cedar, century old cypress, pecans, elms and sycamores." *Author's collection.*

between three hundred and four hundred. Solms then handed leadership of the colony over to John O. Meusebach, who would serve as the organizer, negotiator and political force needed for building the "New Germany" town to be called Comal Springs. It was not named New Braunfels until April 30, 1845, right before Prince Solms returned home to Germany. In anticipation of his new marriage to widow Maria Josephine Sophie, Prince Solms formed plans to build "Sophie's Castle," laying the cornerstone in the new town. When he returned to Germany to collect his new wife, Sophie refused to leave Germany to become a colonist, and Solms never returned to Texas after his marriage to her on December 3, 1845.

Now on their own, the settlers took advantage of the reliable water power, wasting little time in gathering supplies and establishing millworks, craft shops and other businesses that soon made New Braunfels the commercial center of a growing agricultural area.

Many immigrants brought artisanal skills as well as business acumen to their new home. Within a decade of its founding, New Braunfels had emerged as a manufacturing center, supplying wagons, farm implements, leather goods, furniture, beer and clothing. The town also became an important

The original Sophienburg, which was the first seat of government in New Braunfels. A permanent fort and headquarters for the immigration association was built in 1845. *Author's collection.*

Comal Bridge and Dittlinger Roller Mills, New Braunfels, Texas. The mill had several big-name customers, including Montgomery Ward, Sears and J.C. Penney. In 1932, H. Dittlinger Roller Mills began sacking its flour in Blue Bonnet Gingham. The sacks came in many colors and could be made into many different articles of clothing. *Author's collection.*

The Planters and Merchants Mill, Dam and Power Plant, with Stinky Falls running by. *Author's collection.*

market for the expanding agricultural frontier. Its markets supplied places as close as Bastrop and Victoria and as far away as New Orleans and New York—even the Nassau province of Germany. It is reported that in 1850, New Braunfels was the fourth-largest town in Texas.

The community's social and cultural development proceeded with its economic progress. Independent Evangelical Protestant, Lutheran, Methodist and Catholic congregations were formed in the early years of settlement and undertook the construction of permanent church buildings. The initial church school gave way to a city school and then to a district system that in 1858 was incorporated with the New Braunfels Academy. Citizens voted unanimously to impose a tax for the support of a public school eighteen years before the Constitution of 1876 provided for such local taxation throughout Texas. New Braunfels was among the first Texas towns to collect taxes to support schools. Catholics established schools in the 1860s under the direction of the Sisters of Divine Providence.

The much-socialized Germans of New Braunfels organized the Germania Singing Society; the Schuetzen Verein, a shooting club; and one of the early Turnvereins, or athletic clubs. All of these served to maintain the ethnic and cultural identity of the original settlers for later generations. The *Neu Braunfelser Zeitung*, the newspaper that issued its first edition in 1852, was

The public school in New Braunfels. *Author's collection.*

published continuously in German until 1957. It later merged with the English-language newspaper the *New Braunfels Herald.*

By the early 1880s, with a population estimated at 2,000, the community was linked by telegraph and rail lines with Austin and San Antonio, and textile factories along the Comal River were shipping cotton and woolen products. The following decade saw the installation of electric streetlights and the first telephone line through New Braunfels. A permanent county courthouse adjacent to the town square opened in 1898. By 1900, both the International–Great Northern and the Missouri, Kansas and Texas Railroads were providing freight and passenger service and had helped secure the city's future as a manufacturing and shipping center. Flour mills, textile factories and processing plants for construction materials provided the basis for steady growth in the twentieth century. From a population estimated at 3,165 in 1912, the town doubled in size to 6,242 by the onset of the Great Depression.

The Depression and the boll weevil nearly devastated the textile industry, which returned very slowly. A new growth period during and immediately after World War II saw the Depression-era population nearly double again. In 1952, New Braunfels had approximately 12,200 residents. To keep pace with the growth and rapid social changes, New Braunfels reorganized its city government twice in the twentieth century, replacing the original aldermanic

Dittlinger Lime Works and Crush Rock Plant with the International–Great Northern Railroad alongside it. *Author's collection.*

The Comal County Courthouse used contractors Fischer and Lamie. They used stone quarried ten miles north of New Braunfels on land owned by Texas statesman Edward Mandell House to build this courthouse in 1898. The three-and-a-half-story Romanesque structure features rounded pavilion entrances, dramatic massing and superb detail in its stonework. *Author's collection.*

form in 1920 with the mayor-commission system and subsequently replacing that with a council-manager form. In 1947, the city incorporated eight suburbs within its limits.

In the twentieth century, New Braunfels added tourism to its major industries. The replacement of water and steam with electrical power in the late 1800s made land along the Comal and Guadalupe Rivers available for public use. By 1936, the city had reserved much of this land for parks by purchasing Cypress Bend and Landa Parks. Landa Park had first opened in 1899 as a private resort area and was promoted by the International–Great Northern Railroad. It had begun to develop as a tourist destination for weekend excursions from San Antonio. Tourism in New Braunfels accelerated in the decades following World War II, when Interstate Highway 35 was completed and local merchants and investors began to capitalize on the natural and historic attractions offered by the city, especially the recreational potential of the Guadalupe River and Canyon Lake after 1964. The opening of Natural Bridge Caverns and the popular Wurstfest in the early 1960s also facilitated the growth of a tourist industry that by the mid-1980s supported some thirty hotels and motels around the city and Canyon Lake. Tourism had taken hold of this charming picturesque German town, and it never looked back.

The historic Comal Power Plant, which originated in 1925 as a hydroelectric power plant, supplied power not only to the New Braunfels and San Antonio areas but also to every power grid east of the Rocky Mountains. In 1927, it was the largest coal-burning power plant in the world. It switched to natural gas in 1928. *Author's collection.*

When Prince Solms returned to Germany, he resumed his place in the military. In 1846, he left the Austrian service, became a colonel in the Hessian cavalry and later attempted to rejoin the Prussian army but was rejected. He then rejoined the Austrian army and by 1859 was a brigadier general. He fought in the unsuccessful war against Prussia in 1866, in which he was met with defeat as a corps commander. By the time he retired in 1868, he had attained the rank of field marshal. Solms and his wife went on to have five children: Prince Ludwig (1847–1900), Princess Eulalia (1851–1922), Princess Marie (1852–1882), Princess Sophie (1853–1869) and Prince Alexander (1855–1926). Prince Solms passed away on November 13, 1875, and was interred in the city cemetery of Bad Kreuznach. His beloved wife, Sophie, followed him the very next year.

Though Solms had been far removed from Texas when he returned to Germany, the prince never lapsed in his support of the Adelsverein and its goals. Most are unaware that in 1847 he continued to help recruit a group of idealistic young Germans to settle the original land purchased by the society in the Fisher-Miller Land Grant. Many believed that once he left Texas he had given up on his small yet successful colony, but this was opposite from the truth. Prince Solms was destined to be the founder of New Braunfels in the Republic of Texas. In his own time, some people called him a "Texan Don Quixote," while others hailed him as the last knight of the Middle Ages. He may have been restless, impetuous and far from perfect at times, but he was also a unique man of great vision. Prince Carl Solms-Braunfels was much more far-sighted than he was given credit for at the time. He changed the entire character of Texas for the better by his dream of a "New Germany" and bringing the German immigrants to America. As a descendant of these settlers, I can tell you that this is something he will forever be appreciated for.

CHAPTER 1

DUCKY'S SWIMWEAR/ THE NOWOTNY BUCKHORN SALOON

G lancing at the festive-looking shop now known as Ducky's Swimwear and T-shirts may make one skeptical of the building's ghostly history. Its location right next to the Schlitterbahn, the "World's Best Waterpark," gives the building an even more pleasant appearance. With the constant stream of the park's shuttle buses passing in front of the shop, there's an endless echo of laughter and excitement throughout the day. It's rather hard to believe that a building with such a cheerful presence and amusing surroundings could be so gravely haunted. As with anything, one must remember that looks can definitely be deceiving.

In 2008, owner Doug Heilmann purchased and restored the building's historic qualities. He spent countless time, energy and resources to preserve its history, as well as its legends and tales. The owner's finest accomplishment was maintaining its vintage crest, which adorns the roof. Resembling a badge of honor high above the elaborate engravings within the building's façade, it reads "Peter Nowotny Jr. 1903." This silent reminder offers the structure's precise beginning in the pages of New Braunfels' captivating history.

Like all buildings first constructed, one never really knows what the future holds for them. Most will become homes for families to raise their children in, while others will become places of business and some will offer entertainment—and they often switch among these roles through the years. Such is the case of the Nowotny 1903 building. From whiskey to swimwear, it has seen its fair share of goods for sale. Although it has accommodated a number of establishments, none is more captivating than its original beginning as the Buckhorn Saloon.

As soon as you walk in, it doesn't take much to envision what this small-town tavern must have looked like over a century ago. Even though the decor has drastically changed, the design of the interior remains relatively the same. There is no way you can go without noticing the stunning antique wooden floor. With each step, the creak of the floor gives a true sense of being back in time. If you allow your imagination to roam free, you can almost hear the soft muttering of restless patrons hurrying to quench their thirst, the clinking of whiskey glasses and the robust smell of cigars overpowering the room. For any visitor with a strong ability to visualize past images, it seems like a time portal to bygone days. Even for those who are incapable of picturing such make-believe descriptions, it is extremely hard to avoid the strong paranormal presence within this building. It is a difficult thing to ignore, even for skeptics. One cannot help but feel as though they are not alone, which can be rather unnerving, especially when the store is absolutely empty. Most striking are the different characteristics of the eerie presence—as if there were more than one spirit mingling about.

Female employees of Ducky's describe what appears to be the presence of a young woman inside the empty building. As far as any visual sightings, they revealed often seeing manifestations of a shadowy feminine figure appearing. They noticed this in the corners of their eyes, but the minute they turned for a better look, the mysterious form quickly vanished. Though startling at first, her sightings have come to be so frequent that the crew has more or less grown accustomed to her presence. They have even given her a nickname, "Rose," to acknowledge her existence.

For some of the employees though, the strong tingling sensations that would occur when she came near would be a little bit harder to adapt to. When Rose drew near, there would be a sudden awareness of tiny electric currents that would raise the hairs on their arms. This wasn't an unpleasant feeling, but it was unnerving to say the least. Unfortunately, the same female staff members are unable to grow accustomed to what they call the presence of the "mean male spirit."

Every so often, a sudden gloomy feeling would quickly overtake the room, changing the whole atmosphere. The feeling could go from upbeat to a sense of dread in a matter of seconds. This sensation lasted only a brief moment, but it could be alarming enough to get everyone's undivided attention. Things would go flying off the wall as well. Strangely enough, just as quickly as it arrived, it would rapidly disappear. The employees described this peculiar mood change in the room as a battle of the wills being fought between two spirits. They believe this occurs when the bad male spirit shows up but is pushed back by the female spirit. One employee was quoted as saying, "She always wins over him…it's as though she is protecting us. We actually appreciate the female spirit showing up when that happens. We feel safe when she's around."

Surprisingly though, the supernatural encounters described by the staff members were dissimilar from accounts made by owner Heilmann. His paranormal experiences were far more personal than those of his employees. There was a sincere and almost heartfelt tone in his voice when he described his individual chance meetings with the building's ghostly spirits. In spite of what you might think, it was as though he were grateful for their presence. One could even detect from Heilmann a sense of friendship with the ghost that lingered within his building. His supernatural accounts were explained more like quiet protectors watching over him, offering security and comfort. Heilmann even humorously stated, "My shoplifting dealings have definitely been reduced since my invisible security guard showed up." With the employees' and owner's paranormal experiences being so diverse, one can only assume that the building must be home to more than a few spirits. But the big question is "Who were they?" The obvious place to begin would be the name inscribed on the building: Nowotny. After heading to the library, the secrets quickly began to unfold. What is so unbelievable is that the haunting doesn't even begin at the Buckhorn Saloon; it starts with a murder in Hunter, Texas.

The mystery began with a miner named Wenceslaus "Wenzel" Nowotny and his wife, Agnes Soulek. The highly respected and liked Nowotny family originally came to America from Bohemia, Austria, in 1854 and landed at Indianola, Texas. From there, they headed to Comal County and settled in Sattler. Wenzel and Agnes had six sons, the oldest being Peter. Peter and his wife, Christina Rhode, moved to Hunter, Texas, and operated a large farm. The couple's first born was a set of twins named Joseph and Peter Jr. It was these twin sons who would offer a story so heartbreaking it was considered taboo to speak of in Comal County for years to come.

The date was September 10, 1893, in Hunter, Texas. By now, the twins were twenty-five years old. Peter Nowotny Jr. had decided to sway away from his father's farm and open his first place of business called the Hunter Nowotny Saloon. It was an enjoyable place for locals to gather after working at the nearby cotton gin. Unfortunately, on this particular September

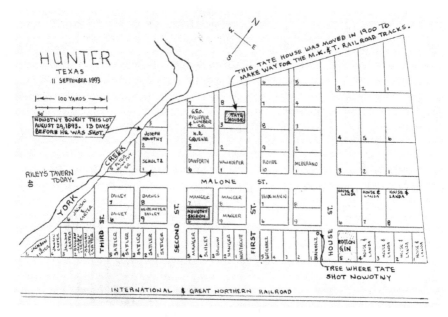

An 1893 map of Hunter, Texas, where Tate shot Joseph Nowotny. Notice the location of the Nowotny Saloon. *Courtesy of New Braunfels Public Library.*.

evening, things would not end so pleasantly. Joseph Nowotny was having a drink in his brother's saloon when an argument began between him and a local named Dick Tate. Their voices grew louder, and the argument became more heated. Suddenly, Dick struck at Joseph but missed and then ran out of the saloon, swearing to kill Joseph someday. Everyone then went about his business with the confidence that this was just another quarrel that would be forgotten the next day.

Around sunrise the next morning, Joseph began walking to his place of work at the cotton gin. Unexpectedly, Dick Tate abruptly ran up to him and began yelling. An argument ensued, and the two men began shouting at each other. Witnesses saw Dick grip a gun, take close aim and fire. Joseph was hit directly in the stomach and fell to the ground. The crowds of bystanders fell silent. Realizing what he had just done, Dick ran away.

Joseph's father was the first to run to his side. They moved him to his twin brother's saloon while they waited for the doctor to arrive. Knowing this was a fatal injury, Joseph's father, mother, wife and brother remained by his side the entire time. He was pronounced dead the next day on September 12, 1893. Tate was convicted of second-degree murder and sentenced to fifteen years in the state penitentiary. He died while still in jail on June 1, 1902.

Because of that ghastly and absurd incident, Peter Nowotny Jr. lost not only his twin brother but also his best friend.

A few days later, Joseph was buried in the Comal Cemetery. Soon after, Peter Nowotny Jr. packed up his family and moved to New Braunfels. The connection between twins has been known to be a powerful bond. Peter's grief was so unbearable that moving away from that memory and starting a new life seemed the only solution.

Peter began experimenting in real estate, automobile sales and even the hotel business. He actually owned the Prince Solms Inn for a brief period but traded it for farmland. It wasn't until 1903 that Peter was to open his Buckhorn Saloon, so named for its masculine and wild game décor. The walls were completely covered with trophy deer mounts, making it a hunting man's sanctuary. Peter was an avid deer hunter and a highly skilled gunman. To maintain his proficiency, he even had a shooting range constructed directly under his saloon for target practice. Although no longer in use today, the firing range can still be accessed through a trapdoor leading to the basement.

Peter had one side of the building fashioned to be used as a grocery store and the other side as the saloon. As you walk inside the building in its present state, you can see the remaining split between the two rooms. This saloon gave way to many good times of drinking and hunting tales. Buckhorn Saloon was a decent place to meet your friends; however, as most saloons did back in the days, it also had its fair share of unscrupulous times. Even with the Buckhorn Saloon's pleasant social atmosphere, it was not immune to such misfortunes. Legend has it that one night another meaningless brawl began between two locals. Bold with drink, the men fought with violent blows, but once they were separated, they both shook hands and then staggered home. The next morning, it was discovered that one of the men involved in the clash had suffered a serious head injury and passed away in his bed. It was to be yet another pointless death etched in Peter Jr.'s memory. The Buckhorn Saloon remained open for several more years but closed its doors in 1918 due to Prohibition. Although Peter Jr. now had to make a career change, many locals believe it was the senseless loss of his brother that caused him to make such a surprising and dramatic one. Around 1919, he was elected as the new sheriff of New Braunfels.

Owning a saloon can definitely toughen one's character. Luckily, that experience was exactly what Peter needed to prepare him for what lay ahead. One of his first assignments would be to safely transport a prisoner accused of a heinous murder by train from New Braunfels to San Antonio.

All he needed to do was transfer him from the local prison to the train once it arrived at the station. While waiting for the train to arrive, an angry lynch mob gathered in front of the jailhouse. Peter had to think fast to stop the furious citizens from causing a deadly riot. He quickly deputized several men he trusted to make the move less obvious. The male prisoner was dressed in women's clothing as a decoy. After hearing the train pull up, Peter opened the front jailhouse door, smiled and nonchalantly walked toward the depot. The angry mob followed him, yelling and demanding the prisoner's release the whole length of the journey. As the shouting crowd walked alongside the calm sheriff, the assistant deputies exited the rear of the jail. They made their way to the depot behind the buildings and placed the female-garbed prisoner on the caboose. It wasn't until the sheriff was securely on the train and it began to take off that the crowd suspected something. With the prisoner safe on board, the mass of furious people ran alongside the train throwing rocks and sticks. It was said that Sheriff Nowotny could be seen simply leaning out an open window grinning as he smoked his cigar. From that day on, Peter was to be known as the sheriff who never needed a gun.

The most horrendous case of his career involved the discovery of a young woman murdered in New Braunfels. The innocent woman's car stalled, and sadly, it was a murderer who came to her rescue. After assaulting and killing her, the murderer dumped her badly mutilated body on the banks of the Comal River, directly behind the once thriving Buckhorn Saloon. This appalling case made headlines in larger cities around Texas, and it was to be Sheriff Nowotny who discovered the body and tracked down the cowardly murderer hiding in a cornfield. This profound case became one of his last before his retirement on January 1, 1931. Many locals believe that it was that case that caused his retirement since the murder had occurred so near his treasured Buckhorn Saloon. Soon after retiring, Nowotny returned to his first love of ranching. It was only six months later, on June 2, 1931, that the sheriff passed away at age sixty-two from a heart attack.

Now after doing the interviews, being armed with confirmed historical facts and given the evidence discovered on the paranormal investigation of the building, it was time to decide who was haunting the old Buckhorn Saloon. With all of the evidence gathered, the collective decision was that there were definitely three spirits lingering in the Nowotny building.

It is believed that the feminine spirit referred to as Rose was the young woman whose body was dumped behind the old Buckhorn Saloon. There is a shared belief that Rose enjoys shopping alongside the customers, helping them pick out the perfect accessory. She delights in interacting with the female staff members as they work throughout their shifts. Rose also protects the staff when the "mean male spirit" comes forth occasionally. This appalling second spirit is the man who murdered young Rose. As farfetched as this may seem, this evil entity has been attached to the building as well. For reasons unknown, his weak spirit fades in and out every so often. His brief appearances are just long enough to express his hatred for women and make known his presence. It is his manifestation that causes the atmosphere of the room to change from pleasant to tense in a matter of seconds. He is the one who makes things fall off the walls, objects on shelves to tumble and items to be moved elsewhere. Ironically, Rose has complete control over him now. As soon as he arrives, she forces him out. In a strange twist of fate, Rose now has more power than her killer. Some like to consider this as life's payback, while others believe it is the strength of a human spirit arising even after death. In any case, he is of no threat to others anymore. The young Rose has got everything under control—she keeps him totally in check, as the employees like to say.

As for the third spirit, the biggest concern was giving the results to the owner Heilmann. Not knowing how it would be received was difficult, but permission was needed before being able to share the truth. Once told the conclusion, he graciously agreed to allow the story to be made public. It was a relief because the account was so profound it needed to be told. On the evening of the scheduled paranormal investigation in the old Buckhorn Saloon, everyone pretty much had an idea who the spirit that continued to stay behind was. All that was needed was some solid evidence, and unsurprisingly, that didn't take long at all to be received. One of the EVP (electronic voice phenomena) questions asked was, "Why do you remain here at this building?" The response on the digital recorder was "Joe." With the interviews, historical research and confirmation captured, a collective decision was almost ready to be made. But one more resource was brought in to validate the conclusion—a psychic.

As she read the building, the psychic confirmed everyone's assumptions. It is indeed Sheriff Nowotny who continues to remain behind. She went on to explain that Peter Jr. stays at his Buckhorn Saloon to continue watching over his treasured building, greet the locals who visit it and carry on his duties as a law enforcer. She chuckled as she indicated, "He despises shoplifters." She then continued by saying, "Oh, and he remains to keep the man company who also lost a close brother. Does that make sense to anyone?" The room grew completely silent, and from that point on, there wasn't a dry eye in the room. Everyone knew this was something the psychic was not aware of because they had kept it to themselves. The day before the investigation, owner Doug Heilmann shared that he had recently lost a sibling. It was not in such a traumatic way that Peter Jr. had lost his, but it was still a great loss of life. This was something that was going to be kept private out of respect for the owner. In that instant, it all made sense, and everything came together.

From the onset of the interview, Heilmann claimed he felt there was always a sympathetic presence near him throughout the day. He believed that it was a caring spirit—almost like having a friendly companion by his side. This was easily established by his tone of voice when he described the occurrences. It is clear that Sheriff Peter Nowotny Jr. is the third and more pronounced spirit that continues to reside at the Buckhorn Saloon. The bond between brothers (especially twins) can be unbreakable at times. It would seem that Peter understood Heilmann's grief wholeheartedly and felt compelled to lend him a caring shoulder. Sheriff Nowotny was an extraordinary man. The highly respected and trusted sheriff had an immensely strong personality. He was described as being clever, kindhearted, witty and caring. This man was devoted to his friends, family and his duties as peace officer. It is of no surprise to anyone that this great man would continue to extend his kindness and responsibilities even after death.

CHAPTER 2

BRAUNTEX THEATRE AND THE CRYING WOMAN

When trying to choose from the vast number of haunted historical buildings in New Braunfels, the Brauntex Theatre wasn't even on the list of potentials. However, when questioning native residents about their knowledge of any known ghostly buildings, everyone referred to the theater. Having a reputation for being haunted was something unknown to outsiders. Evidently, the theater's reputation for ghostly visitors was something only the locals were aware of. It appeared that the hauntings had been kept low-key for years and were rarely spoken of—until recently. When questioned, citizens would give a little shiver, showing their goose bumps, while stating that the theater would not disappoint any ghost hunters. Oddly enough though, no one could provide an explanation for the fear-provoking claims. With the theater having been established in January 1942, it didn't seem old enough to have the opportunity to develop such a spooky paranormal history. There had been no known recollections of unlawful deaths or hostile acts having occurred at the property during its brief existence. For such an eerie place, it had a relatively spotless background. This grand building had been a family-friendly movie theater that offered wholesome films starring actors like John Wayne and Jerry Lewis. Even the first film shown at the grand opening was the clean-cut *Birth of the Blues* with Bing Crosby. This place just didn't seem to be a likely candidate as a haunted building. Nevertheless, locals kept saying, "If you want haunted, head to the Brauntex." So that was the next stop.

As soon as the theater doors open, a theater member is ready to greet guests with abundant hospitality, and on this particular visit, it was to be executive director Jason Irle. As he offered a polite handshake, it was impossible not to notice the gorgeous staircases, Art Deco styling and crystal chandelier behind him. The magnificence appearance of the lobby literally takes your breath away. Trying not to focus so much on the surroundings, the reason for the impromptu visit was quickly mentioned. It was explained that there were tales of this building being extremely haunted, and we asked if he would consider being interviewed. He agreed without hesitation, stating that he had heard the same stories. However, he felt it was necessary to explain that he was fairly new to the theater and also that he was a devoted skeptic but would share what he knew. He also stated that he had never been in the theater after dark.

The interview began with a detailing of the history of the building, which was designed by Dallas architects Jack Corgan and Bill Moore in the Art Modern style. The plans of the Brauntex were inspired by the Washita Theater in Chickasaw, Oklahoma, owned by the Griffith

Brauntex Theatre, circa 1950. *Courtesy of Jason Irle.*

Company. Thankfully, after the theater closed in 1998, it was rescued from years of neglect and flood damage by a group of concerned citizens called the Brauntex Performing Arts Theatre Association, which restored it back to its original beauty. Irle expressed how hard the association had been working on the theater's renovation and the generosity of the volunteers who helped restore the grandness of the theater. The overwhelming sense of pride in their accomplishments and dedication to his position could be felt throughout the whole interview. The restoration of the building was indeed a truly amazing achievement.

After hearing of the splendor of everyone's work, the topic of haunting was next to be discussed. Irle said that the only account he was aware of was the overly obsessed and organized projectionist ghost. It seems there was a projectionist who had worked countless years at the Brauntex who was an excessively organized person. His obsessive-compulsive disorder was probably a result of the projection room being so small—if everything wasn't in its place, it became hard to move about. The projection area even had its own toilet (no walls) right in the middle of the room. When you're a one-mean team, there is no time to take a break for personal needs. He adamantly demanded that his tools never be out of place, dirty or even touched. Everyone knew to never disturb his stuff. After he passed away, the projection machine had been damaged, and the theater hired a repairman who was unskilled in this type of projector. He worked on the machine all through the night but couldn't fix it. Leaving everything tossed about to pick up where he left off later, he went home. The next morning, when he returned, all of the tools he had used had been neatly lined up, dusted off and organized. Astonishingly, the projector was now working in prime order as well. This was to be one of many occurrences to happen within the theater. When Irle was questioned if there was anything else he could add, he mentioned that checking the Internet for a recently released video would be wise. It would appear that this is how the legend of the Brauntex's haunting was exposed to the public. After thanking him for his time, the race to any available computer was on, and the link to the Brauntex haunting video was typed in. Sure enough, it was the computer know-how of several young students that led to the theater's haunting legend extending beyond the local area.

It seems that certain students of a local high school were given the project of developing a brief video to practice their interviewing skills. They chose the topic of uncovering the best place to experience a spooky evening on an upcoming Halloween. After filming nearly the entire school, they made

Brauntex snack bar, circa 1950. *Courtesy of Jason Irle.*

The Main Plaza looking south down San Antonio Street. Notice the Phoenix Saloon on the left (tallest building) and the Brauntex Theatre on the right. *Author's collection.*

the video public on a popular Internet video site, announcing their eerie findings. This unveiling opened a paranormal curiosity floodgate. The results were in, and the Brauntex Theatre was voted the "most haunted place to visit in New Braunfels." With such a daunting label, there had to be more to the hauntings than just a tidy projectionist.

After watching the school's video, viewing an online historic driving and walking tour video confirming the theater's haunting and reading several captivating newspaper articles, the theater quickly made it to the top of the list to be researched for this publication. Obviously, the next step would be interviewing some of the students to determine why they felt so strongly about the building being so haunted. It quickly became obvious that these ghostly accounts had not only been experienced firsthand by these young people but also passed down from their grandparents and parents. Unknown to outsiders, the spirit that roams the Brauntex Theatre has been seen and heard since before the theater's opening. The spirit has even been sadly labeled as the "crying woman."

Sightings of this severely depressed female spirit have been limited mostly to employees closing up the back of the building, visiting entertainers staying late to finish packing and repairmen working through the night after the building had closed. There have been sounds of choking (as if gasping for air), coughing and weeping heard early in the morning. Many believe that this is also when the spirit is at her unhappiest. Nearly everyone who has stumbled upon her manifestation can actually feel her sense of sadness and grief. One local who encountered her presence personally stated, "I feel so sorry for her. It is as if she seeks forgiveness or has lost something. I wish I could just give her a hug." On countless occasions, visitors have felt the depressed female's materialization in the form of a sudden current of freezing air rushing past them, as if she was running down the theater aisle.

Since the Griffith Company purchased the property in 1939, there have been no known deaths on the property—so who is this weeping woman? It is believed that ghosts can remain on the land where previous dwellings were constructed and even roam back and forth between nearby buildings. Such could be the case in this haunting. Before the Brauntex was built, the property was formerly occupied by the Faust Dry Goods Store, owned by the Clemens/Faust family, in the late 1800s. The original lot was granted to Christian Thiel by the German Immigration Company on January 29, 1848. Thereafter, it passed through many hands, including members of the Murchison, Eggeling, Campbell,

Location of the present Brauntex Theatre. The property was formerly occupied by the Faust Dry Goods Store, owned by the Clemens/Faust family in the late 1800s. *Author's collection.*

Paschal, Richardson, Stachely and Tips families and finally William Clemens Jr. In 1894, Clemens donated part of the land to build the First National Bank that still stands today. But all this information doesn't give us the identity of the sobbing female ghost. That discovery would come later, when an article in the newspaper archives was uncovered.

Although the Brauntex didn't open its doors in downtown New Braunfels until January 1942, the land the theater is situated on has seen many visitors. The present Brauntex was originally located next to the passenger station depot built in 1907 by the International–Great Northern (I–GN) Railroad. As early as the 1880s, the community was linked by rail lines with Austin and San Antonio. This hectic depot saw many travelers during its heyday. Most were tourists visiting the private resort areas, many were traveling salesmen and some were convicts being transported from the New Braunfels jail to San Antonio. There was also a large hotel across the railroad tracks that would accommodate these passing visitors. As the story goes, a young unmarried woman had arrived in New Braunfels searching for her beloved sweetheart whose child she was carrying. She had reached her destination by way of the I–GN train and registered at the hotel next to the depot. After searching for hours for the father of her unborn child, she was finally able to locate him to announce the wonderful news. Unfortunately, the man she had been so in love with did not return the same feelings. Sadly, instead of happiness,

International–Great Northern Railroad depot. *Author's collection.*

she was met with anger. He wanted nothing to do with her or the child and claimed that it must belong to another. He then demanded she return home and leave him alone. The unfortunate woman was devastated by his rejection. Confused and distraught, she returned to her hotel room and packed her bags. Having an overwhelming sense of guilt and shame and no one to turn to, she did the unthinkable. The next morning, she was found dead behind the Faust Grocery Store (the present Brauntex). It was determined that she had committed suicide around 2:00 a.m. by way of poisoning. From that day on, sounds of sighing, crying, choking and a deep sense of dread were felt in the area in which she passed. This location would now be where the area of the back stage of the Brauntex is located and exactly where the accounts have been reported. Could this be the "crying woman"?

Since this is the only known horrific account confirmed and it certainly fits with the paranormal accounts reported, most locals believe that this is indeed the same young woman. Many also believe that the finicky projectionist is still keeping tabs on his tools. So if you find yourself sitting in the Brauntex after hours and hear the sounds of tools being clinked about, say "Hi" to the meticulous projectionist. He is merely continuing his devoted duties of caring for the theater. And if you happen to overhear the melancholy echoes of the young woman or sense her despair or the cold breeze of her passing, try not to be alarmed. Remind her that she's no longer alone—the projectionist is watching over the place. Tell her to just sit back and enjoy the show.

CHAPTER 3
KICKIN' K AND THE TINSMITH GHOST

Have you heard the clanging of tools, shuffling of equipment and the banging on the walls in the tinkers building? All one has to do is mention the old Henne Building, known as the original Tinsmith place, to be asked such a question. Since the day this building was first made available for lease, it has been known for unusual sounds, movements and even the smells of a working tinsmith's shop. This is rather odd considering that it hasn't been used for tinsmithing in over a century. One has to only inquire about a possible haunted building to hear about the original Henne Building. And the next statement is always, "But they ain't mean ghosts, just playful."

Although never wicked or malicious and merely frisky and amusing, every tenant notes how widespread the unexplainable accounts are. Many customers, employees and previous owners of the building have experienced the events firsthand. The dealings were never frightening; they were more humorous and entertaining. Never were there feelings of dread or fear within the building—it was actually just the opposite. At times, some of the paranormal versions could be rather annoying, such as the fact that the boutique's dressing room curtains were being fastened before closing only to be found open the next morning. For some reason, the antique cash register still in use was a popular item of amusement for the spirit. Come every morning, employees would find that the register's "no sale" button had been pushed the night before. Often, the main water line under the inside sink had been turned off. Maybe this was just the standard practice of the past tinsmith employee's way of shutting down the store for the evening or just a way to make its presence known. It was never an alarming presence; in fact, the spirit has been helpful a few times. As an example, there was a period during which an employee was positive she had left the back door wide open after closing for the day, but when she rushed back to check on it, the door was tightly locked from the inside.

The history of this building is well known by every local resident, as it is recognized as the oldest continuously operated hardware store in Texas. Also, the next-door addition to the original business is still in operation by the direct descendants of the original founder. Every New Braunfels native knows the landmark called Henne's Hardware because it was and still is the go-to place for everything and has had both a successful and interesting history.

Henne Tin and Sheet Iron (established in 1846) with Henne Hardware to the right. *Author's collection.*

Tinsmith Johann Henne and his wife, Henriette (Deppen) Henne, left their homeland of Germany with their five-year-old son Louis Henne and their four other children seeking a better life in Texas. After a lengthy journey on the sailing vessel *Hercules* accompanied by 152 other German immigrants, they finally reached Galveston, Texas, on August 25, 1845. Henne and his family were transported to Indianola by schooner and made the trying trip to New Braunfels. The following year, in October 1846, Johann bought the lot on which the Louis Henne building still stands for a mere $120. He quickly opened a shop, calling it the Johann Henne Tinsmith Shop, with his oldest son Louis working alongside him as an apprentice.

Using only tin plates, wire, solder and a few simple tools to produce their wares, Henne quickly turned his shop into a thriving business. Johann began by making and repairing candleholders, cups, canteens, cookie cutters, pillboxes and other simple items. Next, he formed objects such as milk pails, basins, cake pans and pie trays. Later, he tackled more complicated pieces such as chandeliers and spouted coffee pots. The Austin Stage Coach Company became one of his biggest customers, as Johann made repairs to stagecoach lamps as often as once a month between 1865 and 1869. For nearly ten years, it was a flourishing tinsmith shop. With the business prospering so much and so swiftly, the growing family was able to purchase a two-story house adjoining the parking lot of the store. Then sadly, in April 1857, Johann Henne passed away at the very young age of forty-nine, leaving his seventeen-year-old son Louis to take over the family business and provide for his mother and six siblings. Although an overwhelming task, Louis took on this hefty responsibility head on. He even changed the company's name to the Louis Henne Company to show his determination.

Unbelievably, the Henne shop survived the difficult years without Johann's help and under the strain of the Civil War's impact. Even having lost one of their own family members to the war (August Henne), the family continued to maintain the store with great strength, allowing it to prosper even under such tough conditions. The shop had grown into an enterprise that began to include other wares besides tin items. Louis Henne eventually invested in a wholesale and retail hardware firm, a dry goods partnership, another hardware partnership in Thorndale, a plumbing shop and a large lumberyard. He even purchased Count Henckel von Donnersmark's hotel and saloon, which was located on the corner of Castell and Mill (now a parking lot across the street from McAdoo's Restaurant). This building served a very important role in early New Braunfels in that it was designated as the first post office. It was

Another view of San Antonio Street, with the Faust Dry Goods Store (Brauntex), the Clemens Bank (still standing), Louis Henne Tinsmith (Kickin' K), Henne's Hardware and the Voeckler pharmacy. Notice the gazebo located in the center of the Main Plaza. *Author's collection.*

Louis Henne's original tinsmith shop, now called Kickin' K. *Photo by the author.*

dismantled in 1904 by Louis Henne, who then used the lot for a customer camp yard for his lumber, hardware and tinning business. The Henne kinfolk have kept this business in their family for generations, and to this day, it is still run by the descendants of the original seventeen-year-old entrepreneur Louis Henne, who died on May 14, 1912.

With everyone knowing of this young man's good character, strength in business and devotion to family and with no skeletons in his closet, it was hard to comprehend why this small tin shop would be so haunted. The present occupant of the building, Kickin' K, was interviewed to make certain that paranormal events are still active. The owner was somewhat apprehensive to be questioned about possible hauntings, but after a few minutes, it was understood that it was only because she was unsure of what she had experienced. This happens quite often—once people realize that they are not alone in their accounts (and that they're not going crazy), it's actually reassuring to them. Bringing comfort to people who have experienced ghost sightings is one of the enjoyable perks of being a paranormal author.

After an extensive discussion, it was obvious that the spirit that continues to roam this building is somewhat content and at ease here. The present store owner has a toddler who frequently gets to visit the boutique. She has been seen talking to the center of an empty room, giggling and smiling as if being kept entertained by an invisible visitor. There is almost a feeling of happiness when the disembodied presence is near, and many get the sense that the spirit enjoys hanging out with the customers. According to locals, there have been countless sounds of clinking, hammering and knocking. This seemed like a no-brainer to everyone. These were obviously the sounds of the tinsmith's work at hand. Since the soft noises were usually heard in the same area, the fascinating sounds are most likely the result of residual energy left from years of hard labor. On several occasions, things would fall off the walls for no reason. As all tinsmiths would often reach for a device or needed tool, it would make sense that an item would occasionally slip out of reach. There were often smells of simmering coals, as if coming from the heat of the tinker's fire as he made minor repairs. This was alarming at first, as it left one wondering if something in the building might be burning. But the aroma would pass as quickly as it entered. When the owner was first asked if an investigation would be allowed in her store, she was a little hesitant. Concerned about disturbing the silent resident, she requested that we not provoke or upset the spirit(s). Once she was convinced that this was not the manner in which the paranormal team conducts its research, she agreed, and the investigation began.

Louis Henne's ad in the *Herald*. *Courtesy of* Herald *newspaper, New Braunfels Public Library Collection.*

Just as expected, every piece of evidence captured by the paranormal team was amusing, humorous and entertaining. One investigator joked, "Why do I feel like I'm in an old-time black-and-white movie starring Abbott and Costello?" When the spirit was asked to return the standard knocking technique of "Shave and a Haircut, Two Bits," it answered every time. On the Ovilus (known to most as the "ghost box"), the repeated words were kind and included phrases like "Howdy," "Never mind," "Got me" and "Goodnight." It even said, "Get out, get out, get out," but it was more in the form of "Let's wrap this thing up!" The findings were in line with what previous witnesses had experienced, and it was confirmed that there was merely one contented ghost lingering about. Almost all of the sounds, smells and a few shadowy figures seen are definitely residual (a strong non-conscious energy) from a lengthy tradition of satisfied customers and hardworking handymen. As for the voices on the ghost box and the items moved about every so often, it is believed to be either one of two things. It's possible that the relaxed spirit may be a past tinsmith employee still watching over the owner's tools and keeping the coals simmering—or it could simply be a satisfied customer, pleased enough with the store's atmosphere that he wished to remain just a little longer.

CHAPTER 4
THE VOELCKER MURDER AND THE COMALTOWN GHOST

It was the largest funeral ever seen in New Braunfels. The local music band, besides a very large number of school children, almost all of the citizens, or whoever could take off to come, came to console the deeply troubled and suffering parents and to pay tribute and convey the last earthly honor to the young innocent victim of a horrible deed. We are convinced that the funeral procession that was accompanied by the muffled tone of the funeral music to the cemetery in Comaltown was at least one and one half miles long. Indeed, every mother present at the grave of this murdered Voelcker child could easily imagine what it would be like if they had a sudden loss of a child by a murderer's hand.
—Neu Braunfelser Zeitung *German newspaper*

This snippet was taken from the newspaper's account of a murder that happened in the center of downtown New Braunfels in the summer of 1874. It was the first of many articles describing the most dreadful episode in the town's era—one that every citizen in or around this small community would never forget. Sadly, this shocking event would also lead to the town's most famous and enduring ghost tale. Being that it was such a horrific killing, this chapter caused a great deal of hesitation on the author's part. Though it is a gruesome and heartbreaking story involving the senseless death of an adolescent and is painful to approach, locals wanted more research on what they see as the aftermath of the murder—a well-known legend called the Comaltown Ghost. It is believed that the female spirit is that of the young Voelcker victim mentioned in the above article.

While some of the ghostly accounts experienced by the people interviewed varied, the young girl's appearance is always the same. She is dressed in late nineteenth-century clothing with curly, shoulder-length hair pulled back with a headband. On quite a few occasions, the demure child has been observed walking a fairly consistent path from East Common Street (near the Comal Cemetery) to West San Antonio Street before the railroad tracks and around Castell Avenue. Several establishments along this route have grown accustomed to her brief visits, as if she was just stopping by for a social call. Sometimes merely standing and smiling, others have witnessed her dancing, waving hello and skipping along the road in the early morning. But if one tries to speak to her, she will simply vanish. Everyone expressed the same feelings that she was not in distress, sad or even lost. In fact, it is quite the opposite. She appears to simply be starting her day in the same manner as any innocent young child would, greeting friends on her way to school and exploring the sights and sounds along the way. To most, she seems like any normal child going about her typical day. But was she the child so many had suspected? This mystery began to unravel quickly once the pages of the 1874 *Zeitung* newspaper were laid open for inspection. The first line of the article began, "A horrible murderous deed has placed our otherwise calm and peace-loving citizens into an extreme state of excitement and the affected family into indescribable distress and grief." The Voelckers' lives would be forever changed from that day forth. The family's name was on the front page from July all the way to the next year with the ongoing details, further examination and the painful trial.

It all began on July 22, 1874, around 1:00 a.m. when a fifteen-year-old boy, Emil Voelcker, heard a loud noise coming from his sister's room that awoke him from a sound sleep. When he entered the room to check on her, he saw a man standing on the other side of her room. The man covered his face and rapidly exited the room, pushing Emil to the floor. When Emil got back on his feet, he could see his twelve-year-old sister Emma lying on a mattress on the floor, a pool of blood under her head. She had received a gaping wound to her forehead from a horrible blow. Emil then turned to look at the bed on the other side of the room and saw their friend Helena Rhodius Faust, wife of druggist William (Wilhem) Faust from Seguin, who was visiting the family at the time. She too had received a hard blow to the head. The frightened young boy screamed for his parents, Julius (Karl) Voelcker (a well-known New Braunfels druggist) and Louisa Karbach Voelcker, who quickly arrived. The horrific cries of the mother could be heard by neighbors from blocks away, including Sheriff Ernest, who quickly dressed and ran to the Voelcker house. When the

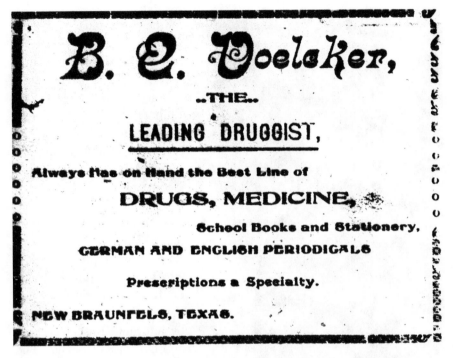

Voelcker Druggist ad in the *Herald*. *Courtesy of* Herald *newspaper, New Braunfels Public Library Collection.*

sheriff entered the home located behind the family's drugstore, he encountered a scene he would never forget. A doctor was called and quickly arrived, but it was too late for young Emma. Within a few hours, she would pass away from the injuries. Although Helena Faust survived, she was to be completely blind forever. News of the attack spread fast, and a posse of twenty men was dispersed in all directions to alert surrounding communities to be watchful of any suspicious persons. The group interrogated strangers and asked the citizens to please maintain order to protect the innocent in the hysteria.

Emma was buried on July 25, 1874, in the Comal Cemetery. Her funeral procession was the largest of that time. Pastor Schuchard, who performed the funeral sermon, read lyrics from the German song "When the Swallows Fly Homeward" to provide comfort for the breaking hearts of everyone present. After the funeral, the mystery of the incident began to intensify, as people spread absurd rumors and accusations that led to several unwarranted arrests and near lynchings. Then, a rather important claim was made that caused great suspicion—William Faust, husband of the victim Helena Faust, was missing. He was now the prime suspect. Helena moved to the home of her

Grave site of Emma Voelcker. *Photo by the author.*

mother, Johanna Rhodius, for safety. After weeks of searching, William was found in Cibolo, immediately arrested and accused of Emma's murder. Thus began the long investigation and trial of the perpetrator, who was unbelievably the surviving victim's husband.

Presiding over the trial was twenty-second district judge John P. White. The state was represented by attorney and future governor of Texas John Ireland, while the accused was represented by attorneys Rust, Goodrich and Douglass of Seguin. The trial quickly became the topic of conversation on everyone's lips for miles around. Now that a suspect had been named, witnesses started to come forward. As the trial progressed and each witness told his or her account of what they had observed William Faust doing and where he had been on the night of the murder, it was growing more and more obvious that the accused was indeed guilty. Throughout everyone's testimony, William Faust remained completely emotionless, masterly controlling any reactions, which seemed impossible for any innocent person. An attorney was quoted as saying, "William Faust's behavior during the trial demonstrated that he either had a heart of steel and knows how to discipline himself in very trying situations, or he is the biggest criminal with a soul as black as the darkest night."

Helena Faust testified that it was her husband who had suggested she sleep at the Voelckers' house that night. Although she refused to believe he had committed the crime and continued to stand by his side, she was able to give her version of the events. It seems that Helena had a dreadful phobia of sleeping alone. Since William was to work through the night in Seguin, he suggested that she sleep at the Voelckers' in New Braunfels. Once she arrived at the Voelckers' home, it was decided that she would sleep in the room of the young Emma Voelcker, who slept on a spare mattress while Helena took her bed. It was this decision that would cause Emma's demise. A witness testified that he had seen William Faust racing back from New Braunfels on horseback during the early morning hours on the night of the murder. He was headed to Seguin's infamous Magnolia Hotel, where he had stolen the horse of the Magnolia Hotel's owner, Rollin Johnson. The murder weapon, an axe covered with blood and nerve fibers, was later discovered in the Guadalupe River and traced back to William Faust. As the incriminating evidence accumulated, so too did the anger. The reality that a friend of the Voelcker family and the husband of the surviving victim had actually carried out such a hideous act was extremely painful for everyone to accept. William Faust had to be moved continuously to avoid being lynched. Finally, on October 22, 1875, after nearly a year of agonizing delay, a guilty verdict was handed down from the jury. Faust's sentence was life in prison. His reaction sickened everyone in the courtroom, as he slowly looked at each of the twelve men on the jury, the judge and then his lawyer before leaning back to light up his final cigar. This cold-blooded response brought chills to all within sight.

For months, Faust had to be moved from one jail to another to avoid irate lynch mobs. Unbelievably, after Faust had been moved to a San Antonio jail, he finally decided to confess to the murder, giving the full details. He admitted that on the night of the murder, he had ridden the stolen horse from Seguin to New Braunfels, arriving around 1:00 a.m. When he entered the Voelcker home, it was his intention to kill only his wife, but the young Emma awoke, and there couldn't be any witnesses. Emil Voelcker walked in before Faust could finish murdering his wife. After the attack, Faust threw the axe in the Guadalupe River, burned his bloody clothes and changed into new clothes. He then rode the stolen horse back to the Magnolia Hotel as quickly as possible, arriving around 5:00 a.m., headed up the hotel stairs to Room #3 and fell fast asleep, believing he would never be caught. He stated that the only mistake he had made was not pretending to help in the search for the murderer. "Had I done that," he said, "all suspicion toward me would have been removed." Astonishingly, Faust went on to admit that this was not his only murder. He had also killed Dr. Rhein in Seguin a few years back over money he had owed him. When asked why he would want to kill his own wife, Faust replied, "My plans were to kill Helena, wait a while to collect her $9,000 inheritance she was to receive from her previous deceased husband in Germany, and then marry her sister. Had the little girl not awakened, I would have gotten away with it."

Several days later, a number of men attempted to break into the jail where Faust was being held but were stopped. The sheriff moved the prisoner to the courthouse and placed him under heavy guard. Nevertheless, on July 28, 1876, between 3:00 and 4:00 a.m., Faust was shot to death through a window. The culprit was never found.

After hearing the details surrounding the murder of young Emma Voelcker, one can see why she is thought to be the wandering Comaltown Ghost. She had been fast asleep the night of her death and unaware of what had happened to her. It was later discovered that she had just returned from her dance class that night, which was something she dearly loved. The child most likely laid her head down to sleep with thoughts of dance steps running through her mind. The trail on which the young spirit has often been seen is the path leading from Emma's home to the Comal Cemetery, where everyone in town walked behind her casket in tears. It is quite possible that this tiny dancer is still performing for her onlookers and welcoming the kind citizens of a town that treasured her presence.

CHAPTER 5
PHOENIX SALOON AND THE SIPPEL SUICIDE

Looking to wet your whistle but hate to drink alone? Then head over to the Phoenix Saloon, where legend has it that one can drink a tall mug of beer while chatting with two of the several spirits that linger there. First, there is one-time proprietor Walter Krause, who was killed in a bar fight. His presence has been noted in the form of bangs, knocks and items being thrown across the room. Maybe he's still participating in a bout of strength, hoping to finally win. Then there is the original owner of the building, John Sippel, whose life was cut short by his own hands in a most shocking manner. John was known to have been available 24/7 to lend a sympathetic ear or provide a caring shoulder to lean on. It is believed by many that had someone offered such solace for him, he might not have committed suicide over one hundred years ago. Today, Sippel silently wanders the building in hopes of protecting his patrons (and especially the present owner) from mental grief, and he tries to keep the laughter rolling. Since this was something he was never able to accomplish for himself, the sounds of music and happiness please him. If you listen carefully, his soft laughter can sometimes be heard in the still of the night.

John (Johann) Valentin Sippel was the son of German merchants Valentin and Anna (Asmann) Sippel, who came to New Braunfels around 1845. Born on February 24, 1850, John was the first of the Sippel family born in America. John's father passed away when he was only fifteen years old, leaving him to become the man of the house and family provider. He would follow in his father's footsteps for a time, working as a clerk and later as

The Phoenix Saloon. Notice the Gebhardt sign on the right. *Courtesy of Ross Fortune.*

a merchant. Sometime around 1873, John met Johanna Gruene (daughter of Ernst and Antonette Kloepper Gruene) and asked her to marry him. Unfortunately, this customarily joyous occasion would eventually become the biggest mistake of his life.

While John was a clerk at a dry goods store and before pledging his vows of marriage to Johanna, he began laying the foundation for a better life for his family. He began by choosing the best setting possible for his innovative plan, which was to be laid out in the heart of downtown New Braunfels on the east corner of West San Antonio Street and Castell Avenue. On December 1, 1871, the *Zietung* newspaper made a big announcement that John Sippel had completed his two-story building, to be called the Phoenix Saloon. This small tavern would become a beacon for thirsty citizens and travelers alike. It also became one of New Braunfels' most notorious buildings, known for its illustrious history and intense hauntings.

The Phoenix Saloon was noted for having the coldest beer in town, which it served in large mugs for only five cents. Live local music could be enjoyed every Saturday night, bringing patrons from miles away. One year after opening, the Schumacher Brewery was established in the building's basement. Although John continued to own the building, a billiard hall was

Looking down San Antonio Street south from the plaza. *Author's collection.*

The Phoenix Saloon. *Courtesy of Ross Fortune.*

added, and in 1873, he began leasing out the saloon to several different proprietors: Hohmann and Meier (1872–73), Hohmann (1873–75), Lorenz "Wusch" Kronkosky (1875–77) and Ludwig (1877–81). During the early 1880s, John Sippel had a bowling alley built onto the rear of the building. These new lanes entertained many of the German bowlers in the area, including the league champion Comal Club 9-Pin team. Unfortunately, it was also during this period that the bar's owner, Walter Krause, was to be involved in a rather uneven fight with a local patron named James Alexander on July 26, 1885. Almost two weeks later, on August 7, Krause would pass away from the severe injuries he sustained during the fight. Many who were present during the altercation claimed that it was an unfair challenge in a battle of strength and completely unnecessary. This is most likely the reason why Krause's spirit is suspected to haunt the building. Inexcusable deaths can often leave souls pondering the loss of life over such a wrongful doing and searching for answers. Sounds that have been captured include those of a scuffle or brawl in action.

After Krause's unnecessary death, the building became the Streuer Saloon (1885–86) and the Ludwig Saloon (1886–93). During this period, the second floor of the building served as the headquarters for the anti-Prohibition movement (1887). The question of prohibition had long been a political topic of discussion, and the small town of New Braunfels was not immune to it. In 1891, undisturbed by the possibility of Prohibition, Sippel built a stone-walled pool that is said to have once contained a twelve-pound blue catfish. He also included an enjoyable flowing fountain on the side of the saloon with a shaded garden area, where ladies could indulge in a cold beer. Back in those days, it would have damaged a lady's reputation to enter a bar, so Sippel installed push-button bells wired to the trees for the ladies to use when they wanted a cold one. Even more unusual was the talking parrot, which sat on a perch just inside the front door and was taught to ask, "Have you paid your bill?" in German. With all the amusing additions to the outside area, the adding of novel entertainment (even badger fighting) and allowing women to partake in pleasures only known to men, many were confused by John Sippel's slowly progressing state of depression. Unbeknownst to most, John's wife had begun to have an affair with a local man who lived on a hill near Landa Park. This turn of events would lead his depression to the point of no return. The majority of John's friends were becoming dreadfully concerned about him.

Although John's mental state was spiraling out of control, his building continued to succeed and prosper. By 1892, William Gebhardt owned and

The café at the Phoenix Saloon. *Courtesy of Ross Fortune.*

operated a small hole-in-the-wall café at the back of Sippel's building. It became very popular with locals overnight. In between serving hungry guests, Gebhardt experimented with exotic new recipes, often trying them out on his regular customers, who always came back for more. Through his experiments, Gebhardt developed the first-ever chili powder (called Tampico Dust) in 1894. It was an overnight success, and he decided to invest in its future. He wasn't content to just serve his regular customers his new recipes (even though they were beating a path to his door)—he wanted everyone to be able to enjoy chili anytime they wanted. Two years later, Willie Gebhardt moved to San Antonio to operate the first commercial establishment to manufacture and sell the newly named chili powder called Gebhardt's Mexican Foods, which is still in existence.

By this time, Johanna Sippel's affair had become blatantly obvious to everyone in New Braunfels. This brought John humiliation and caused him to sink into an even deeper depression. Then, as if to add insult to injury, his prized building suffered a small fire, causing it to temporarily close. When it reopened in 1896, new proprietors Holzmann and Oberkampf hoped to offer John a bit of happiness by naming the remodeled building the Phoenix Saloon in honor of its beginnings. To no one's surprise, this sympathetic act had no effect on John's outlook on life. By now, he had reached a point of no return and was unable to control his emotional and mental stability. This once highly respected businessman had been transformed into an irrational menace, capable of causing harm to himself and possibly others. John had finally snapped, and his life would soon be changed forever.

One evening, as his brazen wife made her way to her lover's home near Landa Park, John followed her. He knew exactly where she was headed. As she entered the single man's home, John took a comfortable spot on the ground to watch the couple's embrace through an open curtain on one of the windows. Having lost all sense of rationality, John then pulled out his loaded revolver and took aim at the couple. He fired numerous rounds, hitting only the building and mercifully missing the pair. Of course, New Braunfels being a small town, everyone near and far began to run toward the gunfire. As chaos ensued, John raced back to the Phoenix Saloon. Knowing that the sheriff would soon be at his doorstep, coupled with the continued shame he would be forced to endure, John then did the unthinkable. Having lost his will to live, on the evening of April 25, 1900, the once esteemed John Sippel placed the small gun to his head and pulled the trigger. He was

John Sippel's grave site in Comal Cemetery. *Photo by the author.*

found dead on the second floor of the Phoenix Saloon from a fatal gunshot wound to the right temple. The town was stunned by the horrible outcome. The ironic result of the senseless incident was that John's wife, Johanna, eventually ended her relationship with her lover and remained unmarried until her own death at age ninety.

Although this act destroyed the life of John Sippel, his beloved Phoenix Saloon remained a thriving establishment for many more years with proprietors such as Carl Luersen and Henry Fischer, Hermann Tolle, Edward Kalies, Otto Reeh, the Alves brothers, twin brothers Bruno and Alfred Pape, Adolf F. Moeller and Henry Warnecke, Emil Mergele, Gustav Becker and Oswald Ulbricht, Charles Scheel, Charles Doeppenschmidt, Edwin Alves and Charles Soechting. On June 26, 1918, Prohibition closed the Phoenix Saloon's doors to the public. But unbeknownst to the authorities, the Phoenix Saloon and its devoted German patrons would not refrain so easily from enjoying their delicious brew. From 1918 to 1922, an illicit brewery operated out of the basement, where two tunnels had been cut under the streets of the town to distribute the illegal booze. These secret tunnels ran from the Phoenix Saloon to several buildings, including the Richter Building, the Brauntex and even Henne's tinsmith shop. The remnants of these tunnels are still visible in the Phoenix Saloon's basement.

The brewery must have been very successful, for in 1922, new owner Albert Robert Ludwig updated the building's architecture and added a third floor. He also added an A.R. Ludwig sign to the top of the structure. The third floor became the site of the illustrious New Braunfels Masonic Lodge for a number of years. Some of the masons' architectural designs have remained, leaving the "hush-hush" society's mark on the town's history. An additional twenty feet was added to the back of the building, and the second floor was transformed into apartments. It is said that many fascinating tales can be told from this lodge's past. But when anyone is asked about its history, the room suddenly grows quiet.

In 1927, Jacob Schmidt bought the building and changed its name to the Schmidt Building, as it remains today. The bottom floor became a department store, changing names several times: Mendolovitz (1923–32), Stehling Brothers (1932–35) and, after a major renovation (including the addition of the first refrigerated drinking water fountain), Jacob Schmidt and Son Department Store (1936–62). After a few insignificant establishments thereafter, the famous Phoenix Saloon remained unchanged and unoccupied until 2008. Then, as luck would have it, the building was stumbled upon by a couple seeking to establish a music venue in Austin. For Ross Fortune and

A 1940 view looking south from the courthouse tower down San Antonio Street. *Author's collection.*

Debbie Smith, the Phoenix was everything they were looking for—except the ghostly resident they were about to inherit.

The anxious entrepreneurs were determined to embrace the building's history as they began to renovate. They used the old department store cabinetry to construct a forty-foot-long bar. The newly revealed original 1871 brick wall told its own story, exposing long-hidden windows and doorways and a few fire-blackened bricks from the small fire that temporarily closed the Phoenix. The pair even found remnants of the old outhouse under the floorboards. The two have tried to recycle every piece of the old building. For the unsuspecting duo though, far more of the building's past was about to be revealed, and in a supernatural manner they never expected.

Even though the new owners didn't believe in spirits, they quickly discovered that it was something they had to accept as true whether they liked it or not. On the second floor, shadows regularly drift past them as they work in the office. Slight chills pass by every so often, and doors slam for no reason. Perhaps most chilling are the footsteps that can be heard when the building is empty. Tightly shut cupboard doors will often be found open the next morning. Evidently, whistling seems to be the ghost's most enjoyable form of communication when no one is paying attention. Ross Fortune is unafraid of the disembodied tenant. To him, it seems more like a game being played on him rather than a vindictive haunting. Fortune even has sympathy for the spirit, as he believes it to be the saddened John Sippel simply longing for the company he had grown so used to. As a saloon owner, Fortune feels as if they have something in common. The third floor of the building is definitely a different experience though. This area, where the Masonic lodge was once housed, seems far more sinister in character.

Having seen pictures fly off the walls and door handles turn when no one is near coupled with the constant feeling that someone is walking behind you is enough to have this room labeled as paranormally unpleasant. The most substantial experience comes on the stairwell leading up to the third floor. It is impossible to ignore the spooky feeling and creepy ice-cold sensation one gets with the feeling that someone is standing alongside you with each step of the way. Several of the employees have even admitted to experiencing a physical touch in the form of a hand on their shoulder. On one occasion, one of the managers had brought down coins to place in the register. He quickly scattered them in the trays and walked away, only to return to witness all of the coins stacked ever so properly in one-dollar increments. With permission from owners Fortune and Smith, the paranormal team members had to come see all this astounding evidence for themselves.

One night, while the bar was still open, the team did a walkthrough in the basement, the second floor and then the third. It was difficult with the loud music being played on the main floor and customers getting into their Texas Two Step. For most of the team members, it seemed highly unlikely that any credible evidence would be captured. But amazingly enough, even with all of the sounds of the band, lively dancing and loud chatter on the main floor, the team was still able to catch some unbelievable paranormal proof. In a matter of seconds, there were indications that the team was not alone on the second floor. In every corner of the room, a loud whistle could be heard, as if someone was trying to distract everyone's attention. Each team member felt the intense sensation of a ghostly presence as they walked the second level, causing the hair on their arms to rise. The instruments used in monitoring potential paranormal activity lit up like a Christmas tree as they walked the area. One of the members was overcome by the emotion of intense sorrow and was forced to leave the building temporarily. This, of course, was the part of the building where John Sippel was known to have regrettably taken his own life. As they made their way toward the third-floor stairwell, the lights began to flicker. Was this a sign to not leave yet or a gesture of happiness for their departure?

As they continued walking up to the third floor, the uneasiness stopped everyone in their path. Reaching the halfway point of the stairs, it was impossible to ignore the change in the atmosphere. The team was well aware that this dense and heavy atmosphere meant that there was an unkind presence among them. They assumed that the feeling of sorrow was the mentally tormented John Sippel, but who could this angry spirit be? Was it Walter Krause, upset with his premature departure at the hands of an irate drunken customer? Could it be from a past Mason troubled by outsiders entering their private territory? There are even rumors of a suspicious death possibly occurring inside the tunnels used to transport the illegal alcohol during Prohibition. Is it conceivable that this person may be trying to explain the reason for his untimely demise? We may never truly know the identity of these disembodied souls lurking among the visitors who step into the Phoenix Saloon for a cold mug of Texas brew. But one thing is certain— they do exist, and they show no signs of leaving anytime soon. After taking on the incredible task of renovating this historical old building, Fortune and Smith were able to restore the grandeur of the Phoenix Saloon in 2010. But unbeknownst to them, by publicly opening the doors to this massive structure, they permitted its haunting past to resurface as well.

CHAPTER 6

NEW BRAUNFELS BREWING COMPANY AND THE BEER— DEVOTED GHOST

Julius Rennart's family was one of the first to settle in New Braunfels, arriving in April 1845. Though he began his career in America as a simple shoemaker, Rennart would eventually become one of New Braunfels' most memorable citizens. He would also be linked to one of the most ghostly legends in the county. Rennart's unexpected popularity would begin shortly after he arrived in Texas, when he discovered that there was no beer to be found anywhere in the community. As a self-respecting member of the Germania Singing Society (well known for singing many melodies over a tall cold brew), he knew this had to be corrected—and fast. With the knowledge that everything needed to create his own tasty beer was readily available—clean water, grain, wagons to import hops, etc.—he began to formulate his own personal recipe. After several attempts, he was able to create one of the best-tasting brews around. In fact, Rennart was widely credited with brewing the very first beer in Texas. Once word got out that he had been able to produce a delicious alcoholic beverage, people began coming from miles around to savor and purchase his delightful German refreshment. This was quite a huge change in professions for the mild-mannered shoemaker, but he quickly learned to savor his newfound success.

With the news spreading quickly and his beer in high demand, Rennart realized that his tiny cottage brewery needed to be enlarged. In 1847, he built a larger brewery on the banks of the Comal River near Stein Court. By 1850, Rennart's trade had grown vastly, causing other settlers to jump on the bandwagon. Within the next five years, there were several breweries in competition with Rennart. In 1855, William A. Menger and Charles Degen even opened a brewery next to the Alamo. But Rennart maintained his

Sponsor of the First Texas Song Festival in New Braunfels, Texas, October 16 and 17, 1853. *Author's collection.*

reputation as one of the best brewers around. Just as these other breweries began to establish themselves, the Civil War brought a halt to production, as ingredients such as hops were harder to come by due to Union blockades. Then, in 1863, much of the local brewing equipment was abruptly confiscated to make saltpeter in Landa Park for gunpowder in an underground gunnery. Most of the breweries were forced to close down, but a determined Rennart somehow managed to stay afloat. Having survived the wrath of the Civil War, Rennart then recruited his oldest son, Otto, to assist him in the brewery. The addition quickly stimulated production of their brew.

Once the war was behind everyone, more than a dozen breweries began to operate in and around New Braunfels. Then, in 1881, the International–Great Northern Railroad linked San Antonio and Austin. The railroad helped create large brewing companies such as Anheuser-Busch, Miller, Pabst, Stroh and Schlitz. Julius Rennart, like many small brewers of the time, felt the pressure of the railroad. By the time the rail link was complete, Rennart was forced to stop selling his local beer altogether. Considering that this brewer was able to maintain his small business for nearly forty years and had survived the ravages of the Civil War and numerous competitions, this was an incredible accomplishment. It was a sad day when Rennart had to close his brewery, but his beer has continued to be remembered as the best beer ever made in New Braunfels. It is said that the loss of his treasured brewery broke his fighting spirit and that he was never the same. Many believed that his grief was the cause of his passing in 1886.

But Rennart should have realized that something as good as his beer would not be gone long, for in August 1914, the New Braunfels Brewing Company picked up Rennart's brewing torch and brewed its first batch of the pleasant local brew. The business, housed in a massive four-story brick structure, was located near the railroad line on North Guenther. Right from the start, employees made note of ghostly sounds coming from the building. Although there would be no one around, there were sounds of soft singing, bottles rattling and the rustling of feet. Some employees stated that they felt as if they had an extra set of invisible employees watching over them as they made the hefty brew. The new brewery reportedly had brewed a beer that was as potent as whiskey. Was it the change in recipe that caused the spirits to interfere? Or was it the delight of a stronger brew that drew them there? The most obvious of the paranormal accounts was the constant rearranging of the equipment, as though the ghosts were making it suitable for their own liking. Many thought the ghost to be that of Julius Rennart himself, happy to be back at work preparing his favorite concoction. As business grew, the company bought out Landa Ice Industry and began manufacturing ice. Afterward, large blocks of ice were often found moved and partially melted for no logical reason. Except for the fact of having a tidy ghost present in the building, all seemed well in the direction the brewery was finally heading until October 12, 1920, when everything changed.

At noon on a regular Tuesday workday, an airplane crashed into the tall New Braunfels Brewing Company structure. Two young pilots from Kelly Field in San Antonio had landed in New Braunfels, eaten lunch and taken off again. But for some unknown reason, the pilots suddenly lost control of the plane, which was headed straight toward the brewery. When it seemed certain that the plane was going to crash, one of the pilots unfastened his safety belt and jumped out, landing safely on the galvanized roof. The other pilot perished when the plane hit the third floor of the brewery. The impact created a large hole, and the heavy motor dropped to the cement floor in a blaze of blue flames. The impact caused major damage to the building at an estimated cost of $8,000. From that point on, the paranormal activity of the building increased, and the structure was seen as cursed by locals. The atmosphere of the building took on a new and unpleasant feeling. The once encouraging sensation surrounding the employees became angry—almost hostile. Some believed it to be the disturbing emotions of the aviator, irate at passing so young or upset by his error in piloting. Others thought it to be Rennart, troubled by another delay in production.

Then, to add salt to the brewery's wound, Prohibition passed. The Eighteenth Amendment made the manufacturing and sale of alcoholic beverages illegal. Trying to save its business, the New Braunfels Brewing Company concocted a weak "near beer" for the public called "Busto" just to stay afloat. The town soon came up with an advertising slogan for the non-alcoholic beverage in hopes of distracting Prohibition agents: "There is no beer near here, but we have near beer here." Unbeknownst to the authorities, the brewery was also illegally producing the good stuff and bootlegging it throughout the community, and speakeasies sprang up everywhere. With the help of the town and the underground tunnels, the New Braunfels Brewing Company continued to brew and deliver its tasty beer. But the overall atmosphere of the building became more and more gloomy. Some descendants of the employees stated that their ancestors claimed to have seen frightening dark shadows roaming throughout the building as they hauled away the illegal drink.

Although able to distract the law for a while, the brewery was unable to avoid being hit by organized crime, which made things even more difficult. Despite last-ditch efforts to save the company with near beer and bootlegged brew, the brewery finally met its match in 1925. Federal agents raided the brewery, claiming that the near beer contained too much alcohol. The agents instantly shut down the plant and destroyed the entire inventory of one hundred barrels. This left the brewery dead in the water. Oddly enough, when the Great Depression set in, the federal government needed money from liquor taxes and quickly repealed Prohibition with the Twenty-first Amendment. On August 19, 1933, a giant parade and dance was held in the streets of New Braunfels celebrating the end of Prohibition. Sadly, the brewery didn't live to see the joyous repeal. By this point, it had been closed and forced to file for voluntary bankruptcy. Prohibition was over, but so was the New Braunfels Brewing Company.

After Prohibition, the building became an ice plant, as home refrigeration was still limited. Local farmers and ranchers would bring their own meats to the ice plant for cold storage. One of the employees began to experiment in the process of smoking his personal stock of meat, and this delectable method suddenly became sought after overnight. From then on, the New Braunfels ice plant turned customers' raw hams and turkeys into delicious hickory-smoked meats. Word spread quickly, and the meat was in demand all throughout Texas. In 1943, the building was transformed into a meat processing plant and became the original New Braunfels Smokehouse. Once again, the ghostly presence that had once roamed the former brewery began to appear, and the incidences were back to being timid and tidy. Things were constantly being rearranged, and the sounds of singing and the thumping of footsteps could be heard late at night. It seems that Rennart was content to switch from beer to beef and is merely keeping his company on the right path as always.

CHAPTER 7

FAUST STREET BRIDGE AND THE GHOST OF THE DROWNING COWBOY

There is nothing more striking than the serenity and natural beauty of Faust Street Bridge. This impressive Whipple truss bridge, built in 1887, towers high above the beautiful Guadalupe River. All you have to do is stand at the center of the bridge to envision the intense history beheld by this wooden passage. If you listen closely, you can even hear the bygone sounds of the long slow-moving wagon trains that crossed the bridge during their extraordinary journeys. Although the bridge was scorched in a fire many years ago, it was saved in the late 1990s and is presently restricted to foot and bicycle traffic only. The unique materials used to build it will always ensure its place in history as one of the most significant bridges in Texas. It also happens to be an amazingly eerie place, as one will often come across the sounds and presence of a weary ghost or two, the clopping of horse hooves, the screeching of a tragic train wreck and the legendary echoes of the heroic cowboy.

Today, if you look down the Guadalupe River's path on any given summer day, you will see nothing but laughing tubers floating along with the current. But if you were to take a step back to the days before the bridge, you would see Native American tribes such as the Karankawa, Tonkawa and Huaco (pronounced like Waco) camping near the banks or a procession of exhausted travelers laden with supplies on their way to the Spanish missions in east Texas. Once reaching the river's edge, the weary travelers were frequently met with extremely dangerous floodwaters, leaving them unable to cross. It would take often take weeks for the waters to draw back, forcing them to

Faust Street Bridge marker. *Photo by the author.*

First crossing at the Guadalupe River Drive. The bridge has since been replaced by a much taller one. *Author's collection.*

make temporary camp. One can only imagine the prolonged monotony of staring at the water's edge hoping for some sign of its decline.

Ignoring the water's fury, some impatient travelers attempted to cross before the floodwaters receded. This mistake led to many lives being senselessly cut short at this location. Legend has it that many years ago, a young girl playing close to the river's edge accidentally slipped into the raging river and was quickly taken away by the current. A nearby cowboy saw the danger the young girl was in and swiftly jumped off his horse and dove into the river to rescue her. He was able to reach the girl and swim her to the safety of the riverbank but had used all his strength and was unable to save himself. His cries of "Save her—someone save her!" could be heard resonating down the river as he was being swept away by the ferocity of the fast-moving current. Sadly, the brave cowboy was never seen again. But it is said that during times of high water on the river, his muffled cries can still be heard.

A more famous and lighthearted story at this crossing involves the aforementioned Prince Solms leading the 228 German pioneer immigrants to New Braunfels in 1845. Upon reaching the Guadalupe River, the pioneers found it too high to cross due to the long winter rains. Prince Solms, perhaps wishing to impress the others with his boldness, plunged into the raging waters and crossed the swollen river on horseback. Although this was incredibly dangerous, he managed to make it to the other side. Not to be outdone by anyone, the brave (and very lucky) Betty Holekamp immediately followed and became the first white woman to cross the Guadalupe on horseback. Needless to say, this did not sit well with the proud prince.

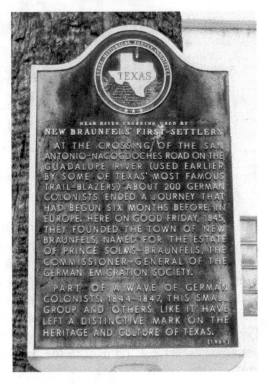

Historical marker near the Guadalupe River crossing. *Photo by the author.*

The cable ferry used to cross the Guadalupe River before the completion of the Faust Street Bridge. *Author's collection.*

For many years after the arrival of the German immigrants, a cable or paddle ferry was used to assist the travelers wishing to make their way across the river unscathed. This worked fine when the river was at a reasonable depth, but unsuspecting flash floods would constantly destroy the ferries, leaving travelers once again stranded on the banks. It wasn't until the late 1880s, when the Comal County commissioners enlisted the King Iron Bridge Company of Ohio to build the Faust Street Bridge over the Guadalupe, that permanent relief was brought to the travelers. It was the first high-water bridge in the county.

At the time of its opening in April 1887, the Faust Street Bridge was one of the first permanent "toll-free" structures completed over a major waterway in Texas. Most major bridges built during that time were constructed by privately funded corporations that charged tolls or fees to cover construction and maintenance expenses. Comal County's investment in the opening of a "free bridge" across the Guadalupe was a testament to the county's prosperity and civic-mindedness at the time. Then again, the Faust Street Bridge was not the only crossing during its time. Looking north up the river from the bridge just beyond Stinky Falls, you will see the Railroad Bridge crossing. This was the International–Great Northern Railroad Bridge and was highly used at the time. On November 5, 1890, a locomotive attempting to cross the bridge was pulled backward as the overloaded and unstable coal cars and the bridge fell into the river. The sounds of the grinding metal, the collapsing of the bridge and the screams of the men on board could be heard for miles. The devastating accident caused the death of the unsuspecting engineer and a railroad fireman, as they were instantly crushed beneath the immense weight of the bridge and steam engine. Today, on quiet, clear evenings, a faint light can sometimes be seen at the bottom of the bridge. Locals believe it to be the light of the fireman's rail lamp. It is

View of the Railroad Bridge and Stinky Falls from the Faust Street Bridge. *Photo by the author.*

also said that the screeching of the train can be heard from time to time, especially on the anniversary of this catastrophic event.

By 1917, the Faust Street Bridge served as the major crossing for all traffic between Austin and San Antonio on what was then known as the Austin–San Antonio post road. Having been traveled by so many during its lifespan and neglected and without proper care by 1934, the bridge had finally fallen out of favor. Instead of repairing the dependable old passage, the county added a concrete bridge alongside it, leaving it to endure even more neglect. A 1979 fire caused by vandals finally damaged the bridge beyond use. But in 1998, the bridge was salvaged and refurbished by caring local historians, who transformed it into a pedestrian bridge. This was also the same year of the horrific "one-hundred-year flood," which caused $1 million in damage and the loss of thirty-one lives.

Although the Guadalupe River had long been known for its unpredictable high waters, it was now being highly publicized and labeled as one of the most flood-prone rivers in America. The locals, who had known this for many years, had learned to respect and observe the river's strength just as much as they enjoyed its beauty. Although the river's wrath is something to be wary of, the soaring bridge is still one of the most serene places to visit in New Braunfels. The Faust Street Bridge is one of the few truss bridges left in the state of Texas constructed prior to 1890. It is also a constant reminder of the path on which many immigrants traveled and the dangers of nature's fury. Listen intently if you get a chance to visit the bridge. If you hear the sounds of the train passing on the restored railroad bridge in the distance, give thought to the innocent men whose lives were suddenly taken away by a shifting rail car. And if you see or hear a courageous cowboy asking about a young girl, ease his worries. Reassure him that his brave act saved her life. Let him know that she went on to have children and grandchildren of her own because of his courageous sacrifice. The story of this rescue was to be shared by the young girl (the author's great-great-grandmother) for generations to come and is still being told today.

CHAPTER 8
DRY COMAL CREEK AND OLD SQUIRE MOESCHEN'S GRUESOME MURDER

New Braunfels is widely known for its extraordinary natural beauty and the calming effects of the river's soothing sounds. Each picture-perfect scene taken in by the human eye seems as though it was created for a postcard setting. After viewing such serenity, one would never expect to come across any displeasing surroundings. Yet there is one area plagued by an overwhelming sense of dread and gloom—a place where the muffled sound of an axe chopping has been heard off in the distance. What is even more unnerving is the fact that this faint chopping occurs only in the middle of the dark night. This legend has been shared by countless hikers and nature lovers who have visited this mysterious area and experienced the sudden sense of despair and hopelessness. Perhaps even creepier is the ice-cold breeze that seems to go right through your body—even on blazing summer days.

This part of the county is laden with trees but is mostly characterized by the steep slopes and native limestone that give a stair-step appearance to the landscape along the creek, as if enticing visitors to enter the woods. The soil in the area is generally dark, stony clay with rock outcroppings, while the vegetation consists primarily of shadowy enduring live oaks and Ashe junipers. Unbelievably, this melancholy section was the site of one of the first communities in the county, known as the Comal Creek Settlement. It was also the location of one of New Braunfels' most gruesome murders.

This grisly story begins with the arrival of J. Christof Moeschen (born in 1806 in Thuringia, Germany) and his family in Texas in 1844. Needing to provide shelter for his wife, Johanna, and their nine-year-old daughter Friederike, Moeschen quickly began building a small log cabin on Comal Creek (now called Dry Comal Creek) consisting of only one room and a porch and surrounded by a cedar-post fence completed in 1845. For the most part, the family of three lived a quiet and happy life, but all that changed in 1854, when the Moeschens' daughter married local shoemaker Carl Riebeling. Friederike's mother favored and approved of the son-in-law, but sadly, Moeschen did not care for him at all. Nevertheless, Hermann Seele, one of New Braunfels' most beloved citizens, performed the joyous wedding for the young couple, with many locals attending. The newlyweds had to begin their future by first living with her parents until they could build their own place. Unfortunately, being unaccustomed to outdoor work, Riebeling soon became very ill and unable to work. Moeschen, being unconvinced of the shoemaker's so-called sudden illness, believed that his son-in-law was merely lazy. Their relationship started off poorly and continued in that disagreeable direction for years thereafter.

It wasn't until the news of a baby that some sign of peace and harmony began to enter the family's future. Everyone was excited about a possible reconciliation and fresh new start with the coming of a new child. Once the baby was born, the family seemed more at ease around each other, and they were content with finally having a more tranquil family atmosphere. Sadly, this happiness was short-lived, as the baby suddenly passed away of natural causes. Moeschen was so distraught about the death of his new grandchild that all of the family harmony was forgotten. Moeschen soon became abusive toward every one of his family members. Friederike grew to hate her father and resented his abusiveness toward her mother and husband. As a result, Johanna Moeschen and the Riebelings contrived a plot to end this abuse and get him out of their lives for good.

One cool, rainy September evening in 1855, Moeschen returned home, exhausted from a long day of work, and began to drink heavily. Moeschen, upon seeing his son-in-law resting in his house after he had put in a full day of hard labor, called Riebeling a useless loafer and then fell asleep in a drunken stupor. In the dark of evening, Friederike provided a bright light so that her husband and mother could kill the drunken abusive man with a newly sharpened axe. After the bloody act had been carried out, the only sounds were the autumn winds blowing through the trees and raindrops hitting the roof. Completely unaffected by what they had just done, they laid Moeschen on a mattress, on which Johanna calmly began to sew him into a bedspread so that no one could see him. The axe was then dropped to the bottom of a recently formed pond near the creek.

The next day, Johanna nonchalantly called to her neighbor G. Holzmann as he was headed to work to say that her husband had died during the night. She handed him a string, which she said was the length of her husband's body, and asked him to give it to Gerhard, who would measure the coffin and make the funeral arrangements. Gerhard then went to Moeschen's home as requested and asked to view the body. The family calmly refused, stating that he had already been sewn into a burial shroud. Gerhard became very suspicious and headed into town to speak with Justice of the Peace Hermann Seele. After hearing his concerns, Seele called for a coroner's inquest. Even though the cause of death remained in question, funeral arrangements continued, and friends began to arrive at the house for the service. Many well-respected and noted citizens were present, including Pastor Eisenlohr of the German Protestant Church (of which the Moeschens and Riebelings were members) and members of the choral society. A carriage containing the empty coffin was prepared to take the body away, but first the inquest had to be performed. The corpse was unwrapped from a dark brown checkered bedspread and then carried outside under a large oak tree and put on a large table. Drs. Remer and Koester prepared to perform the autopsy. The entire crowd was witness to this incredible ghoulish scene. Since it was getting dark, lanterns had to be brought in from town. Even before the autopsy had begun, it was easy to determine that Moeschen had been bludgeoned to death. Both doctors yelled, "The old man Moeschen has been murdered. Arrest those people!" Shocked, everyone turned to the three family members, who were quickly placed under arrest. The crowd, which had been grieving alongside the Moeschen family, was stunned to learn that all three members were killers.

That same night, a ghastly procession of stunned sobbing citizens carried the casket of the murdered Moeschen through the dark woods of Comal Creek as they proceeded to the sheriff's home with the three murderers in tow. In the spring of 1856, all three killers guilty were found guilty and sentenced to nine years' imprisonment with hard labor. Johanna Moeschen died in prison, while Friederike was paroled in 1860 after serving only four years. Her husband was paroled just two years later in 1862.

Was it the unhappy atmosphere of the area that caused the family to go insane? Or was it the cruel family that forever changed the character of the once pleasant woods? Some believe that this section of the county was once a Native American burial ground and that the spirits punished the Moeschen family for disgracing their land. But most believe that the spirits of the murderous family that committed the unthinkable forever changed the mood of the vicinity and continue to seek the peace they never found in that tiny one-room cabin surrounded by a fence of cedar posts.

CHAPTER 9

THE NEW BRAUNFELS COFFEE SHOP AND THE VON COLL MURDER

Entering the aromatic building that is now the New Braunfels Coffee Shop (489 Main Plaza), one would never imagine that this deliciously fragrant place could be so haunted. Yet there have been many nights in the kitchen filled with flying pots and pans and loud, angry pounding coming from empty rooms. Although overshadowed by the famous Schmidt/Plaza Hotel located directly next to it, this building once housed a very prominent person's tavern. This person was an important part of New Braunfels' beginnings, but even more noteworthy was his unbelievable demise. Although the original building, constructed in the 1880s, is long gone, the land is still remembered for being home to the tavern of one of the original Adelsverein council members, Jean Jacques Von Coll (aka Johann Jakob Von Coll).

Born in Wiesbaden in 1814 under the name Johann Jakob, Von Coll was groomed for a career in the Nassau military. In 1841, when he was twenty-seven years old, an outlandish incident changed the entire course of his life. Von Coll and several other officers were attending one of the numerous balls given in Wiesbaden. As usual, there was lots of drinking going on, even continuing into the next day. The officers decided to head over to another party at the house of a neighbor named Schlichter. Shortly afterward, Von Coll was overheard saying, "Let's leave now, this celebration is not for us." Schlichter interpreted these words as meaning that his guests were not good enough for Von Coll. Angry words were exchanged, and one of Von Coll's friends asked him why he allowed Schlichter to insult him. Von Coll sent Lieutenant Sterzing back as a "second" (a peace maker) to talk to his insulter. After a heated dispute between

The famous Schmidt/Plaza Hotel (still standing today), located directly next to Von Coll Tavern, which is now the New Braunfels Coffee Shop (489 Main Plaza). *Author's collection.*

Sterzing and Schlichter, it was decided that a duel was to take place at eleven o'clock that same day. Von Coll tried to come to an agreement with Schlichter, but the pistols were eventually handed out. But since they were unsure exactly who had insulted who first, the two men shook hands and went back to the bar to recover from the ordeal. Later, however, a rumor that Von Coll "chickened out" of the duel reignited the nonsense.

At this point, a military commission was formed to solve the nonsense. The ridiculous affair was becoming very public, and Von Coll feared he would lose his honor as an officer. Duke Adolph of Nassau, who was called to intervene, advised Von Coll that it would be best if he resigned from the Nassau military and volunteered to serve in another country. Fearing a dishonorable discharge, Von Coll quickly resigned. He had only a few choices: Austria (which was not at war), Russia (which he was not comfortable with), Turkey (where he would be forced to become a Muslim) or France. Von Coll chose France, and the duke gave him 1,000 gulden and told him not to come back unless he received a medal of honor. After touring Paris for months, he finally joined the French military, where he learned to speak French fluently. Not long after, he changed his name to Jean Jacques Von Coll. Unfortunately, he became severely ill and was discharged. He arrived home after just six months—penniless, jobless and sick, with no medals. Having not fulfilled his request, Duke Adolph found Von Coll a new challenge: Texas.

The Guadalupe Hotel (later Schmidt's Plaza) with Von Coll Tavern next to it, circa 1858. *Author's collection.*

Main Plaza of New Braunfels around 1906. *Author's collection.*

Von Coll was then hired on as the bookkeeper of the Adelsverein. He even led the first immigrants from the coast of Galveston inland on December 29, 1844. Not only was he the bookkeeper of the council, but he also served as caretaker of supplies, a very important responsibility. Von Coll was most famous for stopping an attempt to change the name of the settlement from New Braunfels to Comal. The immigrants had become very angry that the Adelsverein had not kept all its promises and threatened to change the name against the society's wishes. Von Coll, being guardian of the goods, told the immigrants that provisions would be denied to anyone who voted for the name change. Needless to say, they decided to keep the name after all.

After arriving in New Braunfels and finally settling down, Von Coll married Margareth Schertz on February 4, 1849. The couple went on to have two daughters, Kathinka and Elizabeth. They built their home on Coll Street (named after Von Coll), which still stands across from Carl Schurz School. Von Coll then opened his tavern on the present site of the coffee shop. But a terrible tragedy would soon occur in this very saloon. One day, a disgruntled settler came in complaining loudly about how the Adelsverein was a criminal organization. The irate immigrant continued to rant about how revoltingly the society had treated the settlers. Von Coll, who took great offense to the man's accusations, couldn't stand it any longer. Hoping to simply scare the enraged man, he went to the back and retrieved his pistol. When Von Coll reentered the tavern, the settler lunged at him and attacked him with his knife. When Von Coll raised his arm to defend himself, the settler grabbed the gun and stabbed him to death. Considering what Von Coll had gone through and all that he had done for the town, this proved to be a tragic and meaningless waste of life. Von Coll's wife, Margareth, was left a widow with two small children.

Many believe that the hauntings within the building that now sits on the property that once housed the friendly Von Coll Tavern come from the anger of a man whose life was cut short. In Texas, Von Coll had finally found a place he felt he belonged, and he had devoted so much of his skill, time and effort to helping the immigrants achieve the same goal. One can only imagine his resentment as he took his last breath on the floor of his own tavern, shot by one of the same settlers he fought so hard to help. The owners of the present coffee shop do not fear Von Coll's fury of throwing and moving items on occasion. The ghostly presence has never harmed or frightened them. They have actually learned to live with his wrath and respect his bitterness. One customer was quoted as saying, "When we hear something being thrown, fall or break, we just tell Von Coll to chill out, come sit down and have a cup of joe with us. It seems to calm him down."

CHAPTER 10

LIBERTY BISTRO AND THE OLD CITY HALL BUILDING HAUNT

A fter seeing a video created by a local Comal County tourist site stating that one of the buildings it filmed was haunted, curiosity quickly set in. Interviewing the present owners seemed like the best place to start. This so-called sinister building was said to be located directly across the street from the historical Doeppenschmidt Funeral Home. This definitely added to the fear factor, but the building had its own terrifying claim. Looking at the front of the square brick building, it seems rather simple and plain, with little adornment to call attention to itself. Although the structure appears modest in its architectural design, it is in excellent condition, considering that it's over eighty years old. Still, there is little to note except the large logo of an arm eerily pointing downstairs to the basement. The arm is accompanied by a bright red flaming torch, as if it was lighting the way down. As you follow this unexpected signage directing you downward, you will come to a short stairwell. Unless you've been here before, the entrance makes you wonder whether you're heading into a long-lost dungeon or an actual place of business. As you head to the bottom of the staircase, you can't help feeling curious about what exactly lies beyond the heavy old door. And once you enter the building, the results are both remarkably stunning and eerie at the same time.

This unassuming structure, plain and modest on the outside, houses a beautiful contemporary American restaurant on the inside called the Liberty Bistro. The owners proudly focus their menu on meats and produce from small local farms. Just as the German ancestors did before them, they

The Old City Hall. Liberty Bistro is in the right side basement area. *Author's collection.*

believe in continuing the town's long-lived support of area merchants. As you walk around the dining room, it is interesting to see how each private chamber has been named. There is the Treasury Room, the Senate and House Rooms and the elegant Executive Branch area. Even the restaurant's motto, "Life, Liberty Bistro and the Pursuit of Good Food," has a patriotic sparkle to it. Lining the walls of the corridors are black-and-white pictures of past presidents and distinguished congressmen, giving the room a sense of sophistication and class. Although the décor is magnificent, the question arose as to why they chose a government theme for this hidden bistro treasure. The restaurant owners stated that they felt it was important to tie the history of the relatively unknown yet important building into their business. This all made sense after discovering that the building served as the original New Braunfels City Hall in 1927. But what is even more amazing is the fact that the building's history doesn't begin with city hall or even its construction but with a prince's baker.

The lot on which Old City Hall (now Liberty Bistro) once sat was originally owned by Prince Solm's baker, Heinrich Zuschlag. Zuschlag, born in Germany in 1799, arrived in Texas with his wife, Anna, and two children, Conrad and Helene, in 1844. He was known for the excellent breads and pastries he created for the prince until he headed back to Germany. Zuschlag passed away in 1860, at which time his property changed hands to a man named Goldebagen. Then, in 1868, a twenty-four-year-old named Edouard Naegelin would arrive in New Braunfels and change the flavor of the town forever. Naegelin was born in Alsace-Lorraine in 1844 and was brought to America by his parents when he was two years old. When he was just nineteen, he fought in the Civil War. After the war, he and a partner opened a bakery in San Antonio. It proved an unsatisfactory association for him, so he decided to move on. Naegelin made his way to New Braunfels with only a sack of flour and less than one dollar in his pocket. He would begin his very first bakery in the Goldebagen Building. By 1870, he needed a bigger place and moved his popular bakery to its current location on Seguin Street. His family lived in the upstairs apartment and produced fine baked goods downstairs for more than a century. Naegelin ran the bakery for more than fifty years until his death in 1924. His son, Edouard Jr., and wife, Laura, then took over the bakery operations. The business remained in family hands until the early 1980s, when it was sold to the Granzin family. The Granzins still use the same Naegelin family recipes to this day, and Naegelin's Bakery is the oldest continuously operating bakery in Texas.

Designed by architect and local resident Jeremiah Schmict, construction of the simple Art Deco–style building began in 1927. Schmict also designed the Schleyer Homestead in the Mill Street Historic District 9 (built by local contractor Alfred Herry) in 1928 and was involved in the completion of a jail addition to the present courthouse in 1931.

The city magistrate records were stored in the upstairs of the city hall, while the police department was located in the basement. A walk-in vault was used as a jail many times. It must have been extremely overwhelming for any prisoner placed in this horrific crypt-like cell. Although the building's basement was used as a jail for just a few short years, it housed some famous Texas criminals. The most noted was the violent Rebecca "Becky" Bradley Rogers, a female bank robber. As stated in a Montana newspaper, she resembled a "homely, mild and meek woman on the outside but would probably cut your throat if allowed to get near you." She had actually earned a degree and worked for an attorney at the time of her crime. She was captured after robbing a bank in nearby Buda, and her trial was held in New Braunfels, where she remained in the jail in the Old City Hall until 1934, when a new jail was built at another location.

After World War II came along, the ladies of the Red Cross moved in. Instead of criminals lining the basement, there were dozens of Red Cross volunteers, who met regularly in this dark area of the building and spent hours practicing and studying surgical dressing procedures. It was during this time that the folktales and legends of strange happenings within the basement began to intensify. Several descendants of those same compassionate Red Cross ladies shared their unusual encounters. One of the most common experiences was that of a swift-moving, ice-cold breeze passing right through some of the volunteers, causing them to stop dead in their tracks. This event caused many staff members to leave the post and serve elsewhere. Other accounts include tightly packaged bundles of medical bandages being found tossed about the area as though someone had displayed a fit of rage. This was both frustrating and startling for the Red Cross volunteers, who couldn't understand how this could happen while the building had been locked overnight.

After the war, the building was used as temporary housing for the collection of the Sophienburg Museum while the new museum was being constructed. Many of the items were original documents, artifacts and photos from the original settlers who had founded New Braunfels. Once the museum was completed, the archives were moved to the new museum and the basement was leased to the present tenants, Liberty Bistro. Even before the establishment was completed, paranormal events were well underway. It is said by experienced paranormal investigators that spirits often attach themselves to certain historical items, especially if those items were near and dear to them. Is it possible that spirits once attached to the historical items in the museum's collection decided to remain in the building's basement?

Now that the restaurant is fully complete and doing great business, the accounts have only intensified. Almost every waiter and/or waitress has heard his or her name being called in an empty room. Physical encounters are the most frequent, as the spirit enjoys tapping the employees' shoulders to get their attention when least expecting it. The dark shadows floating across the room have become a daily routine for most of the personnel. Liberty Bistro's most noted disembodied guest is the male apparition that likes to appear in the middle of the Treasury Room and then vanish quickly as soon as you turn to look at him. When interviewing the owners of the bistro, their answer to the question of whether or not the place is haunted was simply, "It is as haunted as they can possibly come."

CHAPTER 11
LANDA PARK AND THE GHOSTS OF MERIWETHER'S SLAVES

B eware of the Landa Park Ghost!" This was a common phrase heard growing up around New Braunfels. It was mostly used by the older children to frighten their younger siblings while playing in the park, and it became a favorite ghost story to tell the youngsters around a late-night campfire. The story goes that if you're walking alone in the park during the evening hours, you can hear footsteps following your every move. The steps are those of the ghosts of the canal laborers, who continue to watch over the hard work that took months to complete. If you step anywhere they feel you shouldn't, they will trip you and then drag you down under the dirt to punish you. You can even hear the digging of dirt and the plowing of the ditch tools. On occasion, you can even see the distant light from their lanterns, as if they're still working throughout the night. Having heard it so often, it was time to get to the bottom of this tale. After some research and questioning several locals about these mysterious canal laborers, I discovered that there really was such a group of workers who dug a canal in the Landa Park area. Unfortunately, I can't prove or disprove their ghosts dragging unsuspecting victims under the soil of the park, but I can explain how the tale began. It seems it all began when a Virginian named William Hunter Meriwether and his large number of slaves came to New Braunfels.

Unfortunately for Meriwether, he will always be known as the "American from Virginia who used his slaves to dig the canal next to Landa Park Drive." He was the principal slave owner in New Braunfels in 1850, owning thirty slaves at one time, according to the 1850 slave schedule census. Although there is no record of Meriwether being cruel in any way to his slaves, he did put them through the extremely hard labor of manually digging an entire canal to run his mills. This is an incredible task to fathom, especially considering the punishing Texas heat. With the majority of the German settlers against slavery, Meriwether was not welcomed into the community with open arms. Nonetheless, he was an American, so the community was forced to accept his ways.

Although unusual for a Virginian to happen upon New Braunfels when most of the settlement was from Germany, it was a logical choice considering that the middle of the 1800s was the beginning of the Industrial Revolution. In 1829, Meriwether purchased the right to build a dam across the Rivanna River in Virginia. In 1846, the year he came to New Braunfels, he sold 150 acres and his interest in the dam and a toll bridge, giving him plenty of money. Having heard of New Braunfels' grand supply of springs, Meriwether brought his experience, wealth and connections with mill owners to the German settlement. In 1847, he purchased a total of 680 acres from Rafael and Maria Garza and the German Emigration Company. The slaves immediately set out digging the canal that would give him the water power needed to run his sawmill, gristmill and gin. He dammed the Los Fontanas geyser springs to create a millrace (canal). Comal Springs, which began above the Landa Estates, originally flowed through the lake area and made a turn going through the spring-fed pool and then under the Elizabeth Street Bridge before going through Schlitterbahn and dumping into the Comal Creek (River). Landa Park Lake was a byproduct of digging the canal. The canal was dug from the spring-fed-pool end of the lake. It parallels Landa Park Drive before going under the bridge into the millpond and out over the falls into the river.

It's almost impossible to imagine how excruciating and backbreaking it must have been to dig out a canal using only a buck scraper, a crude wooden tool pulled by a team of mules. Many of the slaves did not make it through the intense manual labor and long hours. After all that work, in 1859, Meriwether sold his holdings in the Comal Springs Tract to Joseph Landa for $14,000. By now, Meriwether was beginning to age, and his young wife wanted to return to their home in Tennessee. After moving back, Meriwether died the following year. What became of his slaves is unknown, but we do know that they made a significant contribution to the town. Meriwether and his slaves changed the scene forever in New Braunfels with their canal, as it opened up the area for industry. They had no idea that their intense work would lead to such a large benefit to the community. The Landa family would go on to utilize their canal and millpond to develop Landa Industries along with the Comal Power Plant. After changing owners and finally being bought by the City of New Braunfels, much of Meriwether's original property, including the slaves' canal and millpond, has become the beautiful Landa Park we know today. Only one of the original Meriwether structures still stands today—the German import store called Das Spielhaus (playhouse).

Some locals believe in the legend of the canal laborer ghosts, for they have seen and heard them in person. Many have only heard the scary stories passed down by previous generations. Unless you experience them for yourself, you will never really know if they truly do exist. However, the account of thirty slave laborers struggling to complete a canal under the forceful rule of a rich slave owner is very real, and the slaves have finally been acknowledged. Maybe now that they have been recognized, they may rest in peace. Their work will be appreciated for many generations to come and as long as the green exists. Landa Park is a lovely place to visit no matter how it was created, but if you should happen to stumble while walking during the evening hours, just remember—you were warned.

CHAPTER 12

NEW BRAUNFELS' MOST UNCOMMON DOCTOR

The sign on the porch of the local physician's home read, "Doctor, Pharmacist and Baker." But many of the townspeople felt the word "obnoxious" should have been added to this unusual collection of advertisements. According to numerous historical records, this doctor was much disliked by the German settlers, and they tried hard not to use him. Unfortunately, he was the only one around for miles. Early letters written by the immigrants to Prince Carl serve as proof that this doctor made himself largely unpopular right from the start. Of course, this physician would be none other than Dr. Theodore Koester, known as one of the strangest and most unscrupulous general practitioners in Texas. Koester was far more concerned about his political career than the study of medicine, yet he refused to give up his practice. It was said that everyone feared visiting the doctor more than the illness alone.

Koester was born in Frankfurt, Germany, in 1817. While he was attending medical school, it was discovered that Koester's father had fathered a child out of wedlock. His father then forced the unwed mother to give the baby to his childless brother Ferdinand (Koester's uncle) and his wife to nurture as their own. This cruel and uncaring act was something that affected Koester significantly. But it seems Dr. Koester decided to walk the same heartless path as his father in the end. Shortly thereafter, Koester decided to leave his troubles behind him and emigrate from Germany to Texas. The Noble Society desperately needed a physician, so he was quickly hired by the Adelsverein to be the doctor for the immigrants aboard the ship and in the settlement. He left on the first ship, the *Johann Dethardt*. Immigrant Carl Elmendorf was the first to write a complaint, stating that Koester had made insulting remarks toward women and had even made fun of a feeble-minded man. He said that Koester became drunk when they landed in Galveston, despite the fact that they had all been warned about the possibility of strong alcohol in Texas. This was certainly a bad start in the eyes of the settlers.

Another immigrant, Philipp Luck, wrote that his pregnant wife had gone into labor while at camp and that Koester had said that she was "faking it." Luck eventually found a midwife three miles away to deliver the baby. Immigrant Adam Voigt stated that Koester had called his wife insulting names while he was examining her. The prince, bowing to the complaints of the settlers, suspended Koester, but only for a temporary period. For unknown reasons, Dr. Koester was quickly reinstated. Perhaps any doctor was better than none. In his *A Sojourn in Texas 1846–1847*, Alwin Sörgel writes of Koester, "It is difficult to say whether his unscrupulousness comes from his ignorance or vice-versa. At this time, they are waiting to confirm his next poisoning so he can be removed and brought to trial or he will be lynched." According to some accounts, Koester ministered to the sick, but other accounts suggest that he buried most of his patients. Survivors called the cemetery "Koester's Plantation." Even with all the bad rumors roaming around town, Koester had no intentions of quitting—he even purchased a lot on the corner of Seguin and Garden Streets.

In 1846, Koester married immigrant Sophie Tolle. The couple had seven children: Emma, Elise, Harry, Mary, Willie, Friedrich and Anna. To accommodate the growing family, a large two-story house with a basement (still standing today) was built in 1859. The house was unusually elaborate for its time. Local architect W.A. Thielepape constructed the building of cedar, oak and limestone. The kitchen was located in the basement, and food was carried to the dining room on the first floor by a dumbwaiter. The doctor's office was also on the first floor, with bedrooms located on the second floor. All three floors were connected by a winding stairway with speaker tubes. In spite of the complaints about his medical practice, Koester seemed to enjoy political popularity. Proof of that came when he was elected city alderman in 1846. Some hoped that he'd quit his practice and move on. Later, Comal County citizens were called upon to elect two delegates to represent the county at the convention in Austin to decide whether Texas should secede from the Union. Koester was elected (most likely to get him out of town) along with Walter Preston. Koester was also a successful businessman, operating a paper factory, a distillery and a woolen mill. Koester died at the age of sixty and was buried in the Adelsverein Cemetery. Sophie went to live with her married daughter, Marie Eisenlohr, in Dallas.

Although there are no known tales or legends of Dr. Koester remaining in New Braunfels to haunt, it was important to share the history of his unusual medical practice, as many of his patients passed from questionable causes. If you have an ancestor whose death certificate was signed by Dr. Koester, you might want to do some thorough research—the cause of death might not be as accurate as you would think.

CHAPTER 13

MYRON'S STEAKHOUSE / MA'S CAFÉ

Myron's Prime Steakhouse was actually the main inspiration in pursuing this publication, as it was the first location visited after researching haunted places in New Braunfels. The interview began rather awkwardly, as it was the very first ghost conversation with an owner, and we were both nervous. Since it was such a sophisticated establishment, bringing up the subject of possible ghost hauntings was rather challenging. It was even more difficult having known that family members had spent many hours at this exquisite restaurant. But after the discussion began, it didn't take long to realize that this was indeed the perfect place to start. From the beginning, everything seemed to just fall into place. The owner, Bill Been, and his friendly employees were so accommodating and eager to speak of their unusual paranormal accounts. Their ghostly accounts also had backing from the Ripcrew Paranormal Team, which had also determined that the building was haunted. The team had just completed an investigation for the owner due to high levels of paranormal activity, and the results were incredible. Once its analysis was complete, the team's conclusion was that the building was unquestionably haunted. The members collected and provided as evidence numerous audio and video clips that would send chills down anyone's spine.

During the day, this establishment is a fabulous and impressive steakhouse. But come nightfall, this seemingly quiet building becomes one of the spookiest places in New Braunfels. Even the staff members are afraid to be left alone for an extended amount of time. The building's mysterious history, the paranormal team's evidence and the positive support from the owner to pursue such a book gave this publication a desperately needed boost.

This elegant steakhouse, located in the historic downtown district of New Braunfels at 136 North Castell Avenue, is tucked away in an unusual setting. If you look carefully enough at its exterior, you might be able to guess the original purpose of the building. This presently stylish building got its start as the modest Palace Movie Theatre. The uniquely shaped box office still stands at the front of the building. The grand opening of this short-lived theater was held on December 23, 1924. At that time, there were several theaters in the area, and the Palace never became as popular as the Rialto, Cole or Brauntex. For some reason, the theater wasn't received by the public with much enthusiasm. It's possible that there were already too many theaters available at the time, causing too much competition. Whatever the reason, the theater didn't have much of a chance to succeed. Although the building's cinema architecture is still very noticeable, its history is not as obvious. The area that originally served as the main seating area of the movie house is where most of the paranormal activity occurs. The most common sighting is the apparition of a cowboy who likes to sit in the top row. This brawny man, with his cowboy boots, hat and spurs, can be seen lodging during the early hours of the morning. He has often been seen sitting in one of the old theater chairs, as if he was simply waiting for the show to begin. He is certainly considered one of the more relaxed ghosts in town. Every so often, the clicking of his spurs and stomping of his boots can be heard, as if he was just taking a walk. Maybe the theater was a favorite stopping-off point when passing through town—or maybe it's the drowning cowboy ghost looking for comfort in a short film. It could even be a lonesome ranch hand who passed away nearby on his trail to San Antonio. Who knows?

When the theater closed in 1932, it became the popular Ma's Café. This is what most of the locals remember the building as before Myron's was established. Very few locals know that Myron's was once a theater, even though that is what the historical marker boasts about. The original Ma's Café opened in 1912 under the name Fritz Bloedorn Restaurant at 194 West San Antonio Street. The owners were Fritz and Milda "Ma" Bloedorn. The couple had two children, Arthur and Erna, and also operated a boardinghouse upstairs. After Milda and Fritz divorced, the restaurant was moved to the old Palace Theatre building in 1935, and the name was changed to Ma's Café. Everyone would go to eat and drink morning coffee in this small establishment, and it was said that Ma made the best biscuits in town. At one time, there was a popular beauty salon located next to the café. Many husbands spent hours eating, talking and waiting in the café while their wives had their hair done. The most hilarious memory passed down through the generations was that of the rather hefty accordion player who used to entertain the café customers while they ate. The large musician would bellow out a charming German song or two and amuse the clients with his funny wobbling dance all night long. Ma continued to run her delightful business until 1961, when she handed the torch to her son, Arthur "Schimmel" Bloedorn. Arthur kept the place going until 1980, when he finally closed the doors and sold the building.

Not long after Myron's Steakhouse opened, the paranormal activity began to increase. What is so amazing is that the ghostly accounts are similar to what one would expect to hear and see if visiting the old Ma's Café. Melodic sounds resembling accordion music have been heard, and dance steps can be heard on the floors above. Most frustrating for the restaurant staff is the constant moving of the napkins from one table to another. For some unknown reason, the spirit(s) like to have the coffee cups arranged on the tables right side up instead of upside down. Most believe that it's just Ma changing the table settings to her own liking, while others believe it is the jovial musician still entertaining the crowd. But one thing is certain: the ghosts that continue to linger in Myron's restaurant are of no threat to anyone—if anything, they're amusing. Staff members, customers and many locals feel that it is simply the residual effects of many happy hours spent watching movies of days gone by and the cheery atmosphere of Ma's Café. But Myron's will always leave you with a wonderful taste in your mouth, as well as that unanswered question of whether or not ghosts really do exist. If they do, you'll find them in New Braunfels.

CHAPTER 14

COMAL COUNTY COURTHOUSE AND THE GHOST EMPLOYEE

It would seem that for some, if you like your job enough, it would be hard to let go even when you're dead. Evidently, that is exactly what has happened at the Comal County Courthouse. Staff members at the office said that many years ago, a longtime employee had to be forcibly removed by the sheriff and his deputies. Now that she has finally passed away, she has returned to the courthouse. And this time, they can't force her to leave.

The ghostly employee has been said to drive the employees nuts at times with all the strange things that she does. One current employee who had gone up to the attic to put away some papers found that the attic light had been left on. Upset that someone had been so careless, she yelled down below in frustration. Then in an instant, the lights went out, and no one was near the light switch.

The ghost is lovingly called Irene, as many believe it to be the late Comal County clerk of the same name who worked there in the early 1980s. Many employees will come into work only to discover that their computers have already been turned on, the heights of their chairs readjusted and items on their desks moved about. In the early morning, while it's still dark, custodians have heard groans and footsteps throughout the building. Staff members insist that the past employee isn't impressed with the technology and modernization of the office so she continues to mess it up. The office records are continuously being tampered with, as one of the employees discovered firsthand. The employee, who was working late by himself, had a

The Main Plaza in New Braunfels. The courthouse is still standing, but the cannon used to protect the town has since been removed. *Author's collection.*

This is a bird's-eye view from the courthouse. The building to the left was a local department store that eventually burned down and became a parking lot for the current bank next to Naegelin's. *Author's collection.*

pile of papers stacked on his desk that he was getting ready to throw away. Then suddenly, the papers went flying off his desk for no reason. As he was leaving the office that night, he felt the hair on the back of his neck stand up as he heard someone walking behind him. When he turned around, there

The Comal County Courthouse with the Landa Mansion (now gone) to the right. Notice that the fountain had not been installed yet. *Author's collection.*

was no one to be found. The most frightening accounts come in the form of movements seen in the corner of one's eye when alone, as if a shadow has just passed. The spirit likes to make her presence felt often, according to the workers. An apparition of a female ghost wearing a pink dress has even been seen walking in the hallway outside of certain employees' offices. The employees have grown used to the spirit's presence. To them, it's simply an ex-employee who loved her job and always made certain that everything was done correctly. She only wishes to continue doing what she did best—and that was being in charge.

CHAPTER 15

AUTHOR'S CONCLUSION

Writing a book about the history and hauntings of specific buildings and places really makes one think. Having felt that chill along the spine sending goose bumps all over, the feeling of dread and that sudden drop in temperature really makes an impact. These are signs that most paranormal investigators equate with a ghostly presence. But how do these buildings, parks and public places become haunted? Some of these places harbored well-known ghostly residents with extensive pasts that gave clues as to why their spirits lingered in that particular place. Possibilities include wrongful or accidental deaths and betrayal by a dear loved one. Many places, such as prisons, hotels and, of course, cemeteries, tend to attract ghosts simply because of their history and what they are. But some of the most common haunts may not have such a specific story. Why do they remain?

Each individual person is unique in his or her own personality and experiences. Because of this, the imprint (spirit, ghost, etc.) of the deceased retains these specialized factors if he or she is unable to move on after death. The unique characteristics of each person and their haunting locations are different. There are many different factors to consider in determining the reason why a location is haunted. Many paranormal investigators believe that limestone is like a magnet for spirits. Some say that the power and energy of a river's current draws spirits in. A few believe that it is simply the power or energy of the spirit that allows it to remain. The truth is that each haunted location is different and each ghost unique. But one thing is certain: bad events or intense situations increase the probability of a place being haunted. One who leaves under normal circumstances seems to have no problem crossing over to the other side. But those at the center of such ill-fated occurrences feel bound to this world until they receive some form of justice, retribution or simply acknowledgement of their personal stories of sorrow.

Violent deaths, cruelty and abuse are some of the most prominent events that bind a ghost to the earthly realm. But other situations, such as severe unhappiness, betrayal by someone dear to their hearts and even intense sickness, can lead to ghosts feeling that they cannot move on. All of these traits cling to a location—whether in the walls of a building or the soil of the ground itself—to leave a certain ghostly energy or impression. Battlegrounds in particular, where blood has actually soaked into the ground, can create a spiritual residue on which unsettled ghostly beings can manifest and linger on the land itself and even on structures that are later built on the historically bloodstained ground. But human pain and suffering are the major factors that tend to dictate whether a location will become haunted or not.

There aren't many ghost stories centered in sporting arenas or theme parks, and this rarity in hauntings links to the fact that those places usually lack pain and are, in fact, filled with happiness and excited emotions. Many spirits haunt places where their personal pain was thought to be the greatest, but occasionally, spirits will exist in places of general pain and suffering that were a part of their lives in some way. Ghosts tend to keep to places that they considered their own during their former lives or areas they were once very closely linked to. Professional investigators know very well that ghosts make noises or movements to make their presence known to the living or because they are particularly upset at the time, linking to the very human aspect of mood swings. Most ghosts try to reveal themselves in a form that resembles the figure they held in life so that the living can see them as they once were. It's believed that the spirits hope to impress the vivid memories that are holding them to the physical realm. This desire to make known to the living their past hardships and uncommon problems or issues leads to ghosts revealing themselves to all kinds of people, including both skeptics and believers.

Some of the most vivid haunting examples take place in haunted houses. There are several reasons why these home-based tales are the most intense, even though statistical investigations show that houses are very low on the list of places that can be frequently haunted by spirits. Like the saying goes, "Home is where the heart is." And home is often where these ghosts feel safest. But for the living, home is our retreat and personal refuge, and the presence of an angry spiritual entity in our private and fortified space obviously makes us very scared and intimidated. But pure numbers tell us that ghosts actually tend to avoid homes in preference of other locations. Ghosts need a great deal of energy in an area in order to materialize, and personal houses do not offer enough energy to make manifestation easily possible. Larger places that attract a greater number of people—hotels, cemeteries, museums, churches, ships or even dance/music clubs—supply more emotional energy in the air for ghosts to use, making them better choices than houses.

So why do ghosts exist? As of right now, there is no one answer, and that is the reason there will continue to be paranormal investigators, documentaries and books on hauntings. Until we discover a way to stop a spirit from remaining after a horrible ordeal or learn how to assist in helping a spirit move on, there will continue to be haunted locations with ghosts only wishing to find answers.

BIBLIOGRAPHY

Biesele, Rudolph Leopold. *The History of the German Settlements in Texas, 1831–1861*. Waco, TX: Eakin Press, 1987.

Geue, Chester W., and Ethel Hander Geue. *A New Land Beckoned: German Immigration to Texas 1844–1847*. Waco, TX: Texian Press, 1972.

Haas, Oscar. *History of New Braunfels and Comal County, Texas, 1844–1946*. 1983. Austin, TX: Steck Company, 1968. Reprint, 1983.

Horn, Tammy. *Bees in America: How the Honey Bee Shaped a Nation*. Lexington: University Press of Kentucky, 2005.

Johnson, David, and Rick Miller. *The Mason County "Hoo Doo" War, 1874–1902*. Denton: University of North Texas Press, 2009.

Kattner, Lauren Ann. "From Immigrant Settlement into Town: New Braunfels, Texas, 1845–1870." *American Studies* 36 (1991): 155–77.

King, Irene Marschall. *John O. Meusebach*. Austin: University of Texas Press, 1967.

Lich, Glen E. *The German Texans*. Austin: University of Texas Press, 1996.

Morgenthaler, Jefferson. *The German Settlement of the Texas Hill Country*. Boerne, TX: Mockingbird Books, 2007.

Solms, Carl, Theodore G. Gish and Wolfram M. Von-Maszweski. *Voyage to North America, 1844–1845: Prince Carl of Solms' Texas Diary of People, Places, and Events*. Denton: University of North Texas Press, 2000.

INTERNET SOURCES

Ancestry.com: http://www.ancestry.com.
New Braunfels Footprints in Time Historic Walking and Driving Tours: http://nbfootprintsintime.com.
New Braunfels Info: http://www.newbraunfelsinfo.com.
New Braunfels Smokehouse (History): http://www.nbsmokehouse.com/about/history.
Sophienburg Museum and Archives: http://www.sophienburg.org.
Texas State Historical Association: http://www.tshaonline.org.

ABOUT THE AUTHOR

Erin O. Wallace wears a coat of many colors in her profession. She is the published author of *Central Texas Paranormal Society: Their History and Haunted Experiences*. This was her first experience in dealing with the paranormal realm, and it only left her wanting more. She is the owner of the SerinGhedi Talent and Social Media Agency, coordinator for Texas Paranormal Events, historical researcher for Gravel Productions, guest coordinator for the *Paranormal Mayhem Zone (PMZ)* radio show, graphic artist, freelance writer and professional genealogical researcher. Wallace is an award-winning history writer and syndicated genealogical columnist specializing in newspaper and magazine articles. Her numerous affiliations include: Otis House State

Photo by Kay Taylor.

Museum (curator), St. Tammany Parish Genealogical Society, St. Tammany Historical Society, Council of Genealogical Columnist (third place in the

About the Author

1998 Excellence in Writing Competition), Maritime Museum Society and the Louisiana State Library and Archives (researcher). She is a fifth-generation Texan, born and raised in San Antonio. She is a mother of two and grandmother of one. As a child, her grandmother shared the many stories of her German ancestors, Zuercher (Zurcher), one of the founding families of New Braunfels, Texas. She learned of their struggles and hardships as early settlers. It was those memories that guided her to become a local historian and syndicated genealogical columnist.

Printed in the USA
CPSIA information can be obtained
at www.ICGtesting.com
LVHW020845151123
763853LV00019B/22